THRU TRAFFIC
NEXT EXIT 3 MILES

EXIT 13A
Newark Airport
Elizabeth Seaport

# Uncle John's
## PLUNGES INTO
# New Jersey

PORTABLE
PRESS

Ashland, Oregon

UNCLE JOHN'S PLUNGES INTO NEW JERSEY

Copyright © 2015 Portable Press

Portable Press is an imprint of the Printers Row Publishing Group
A Division of Readerlink Distribution Services, LLC

"Bathroom Reader," "Portable Press," and "Bathroom Readers' Institute" are registered trademarks of Readerlink Distribution Services, LLC. All rights reserved.

For information, write:
The Bathroom Readers' Institute, P.O. Box 1117, Ashland, OR 97520
www.bathroomreader.com • e-mail: mail@bathroomreader.com

The Bathroom Readers' Institute would like to thank the following people whose advice and assistance made this book possible:

| | | |
|---|---|---|
| Gordon Javna | Jo Walton | William Dylan Powell |
| JoAnn Padgett | Dan Mansfield | John Scalzi |
| Melinda Allman | Jenness Crawford | Susan Steiner |
| J. Carroll | Debbie Hardin | Peter Norton |
| Amy Briggs | Kerry Kern | Sydney Stanley |
| Tina Vaughan | Lea Markson | Sean Moore |
| Adam Moore | Kathleen McCabe | Blake Mitchum |
| Philippa Baile | Debbie Pawlak | Aaron Guzman |

Cover design by Rusty von Dyl • Interior layout and design by Moseley Road

Library of Congress Cataloging-in-Publication Data

Uncle John's plunges into New Jersey. -- Illustrated edition.
    pages cm
    ISBN 978-1-62686-113-8 (hardcover)
1.  New Jersey--Miscellanea. 2.  New Jersey--Humor.  I. Bathroom Readers'
Institute.
(Ashland, Or.)  II. Title. III. Title: Plunges into New Jersey.
    F134.6.U53 2014
    974.9--dc23

                                    2013043001

Printed in China
First Printing
19 18 17 16 15   1 2 3 4 5

# Contents

# Introduction

## Welcome to the Garden State

Which super-small state offers a super-sized variety of people, places, and festivities? Hint: It's so idyllic that it has towns named Pleasantville and Maple Shade, but it's also got the hustle and bustle of Atlantic City and Hoboken—the Most Exciting Small City in America (really). Yes, we're talking about you, New Jersey!

From its forests to its beaches, its lighthouses to its haunted houses, its celebrated traditions to its secret past, there's so much to say about this small state because it's got so much character. That's why we at the Bathroom Readers' Institute decided to give New Jersey its own book. If you're familiar with Uncle John's Bathroom Reader series, you'll know to expect the most off-the-wall trivia, funny news, fun facts, clever quotes, and stuff that makes you go "Huh?" But we've added something special to this edition—hundreds of full-color photos and illustrations. They make the stories shine and bring to life the Garden State's colorful, in-your-face personality. So buckle up and get ready for a wild ride. This book is your ticket to…

**Meet the People**. Misbehaving mayors, sports Hall of Famers, heroes and villains of Prohibition (we'll let you decide who's who), and the woman who risked everything during the Revolutionary War…to save her horse.

**Eat and Drink.** Get the scoop on Campbell's soup, savor saltwater taffy's sweet history, and behold the return of New Jersey's own India Pale Ale.

**Be Merry.** Witness the first-ever college football game, find out which Kevin Smith movie earned an NC-17 rating (and why), tour familiar hangouts from *The Sopranos* and *Boardwalk Empire*, and jam with Count Basie, Bon Jovi, and the Boss.

**Plunge into Mystery.** Who kidnapped the Lindbergh baby? What caused the S.S. *Morro Castle* to explode and kill 134 people? And what's the deal with the Jersey Devil?

**Marvel at the Wildlife.** Watch quietly as flying squirrels go nuts, an anaconda is hunted in Hopatcong, Bridgeton's coatimundi predicts the weather, and horseshoe crabs overrun the Shore during mating season—which we hear is even more wild than spring break.

**Get Weird.** Laugh at New Jersey's looniest laws, snicker at Princeton's Nude Olympics, and see the world's largest collection of spoons, a one-legged giant, and robot musicians made from car parts.

But before you head down the Turnpike, just one quick detour: We'd like to thank the terrific team whose incredible passion for the great Garden State made this book possible. We're as full of appreciation as New Jersey is full of people. And now, gear up for fun on the pages ahead.

And as always…

*Go with the flow!*

**—Uncle John and the BRI staff**

*Facing page: The George Washington Bridge glows at night.*

# The Basics

*Quick! Let's get to know the Garden State.*

## Welcome to New Jersey

- New Jersey's capital is Trenton.

- Its largest city is Newark. Population: 277,727.

- The state's total population is about 8.8 million. New Jersey is densely populated, averaging about 1,197 people per square mile.

- Two types of poisonous snakes call the Garden State home: The northern copperhead can be found in North Jersey, and the timber rattlesnake lives in both the northern and Pinelands regions.

- New Jersey has some wild critters in its woods: coyotes, eagles, and bears all live among us!

*New Jersey's highest point*

- The state's highest elevation is at High Point, located on the Kittatinny Ridge in Sussex County. In High Point State Park, there's a 221-foot-tall obelisk that serves both as a veterans memorial and the state's highest point, 1,803 feet above sea level.

- The fastest (legal) speed limit on any New Jersey highway is 65 mph. But if drivers go even 10 mph over that posted limit, they can be charged double fines.

- New Jersey is the only state without an official song, but it does have an unofficial one. In 1972, the state legislature declared "I'm from New Jersey," written by a Phillipsburg man named Red Mascara (birth name: Joseph Rocco Mascari), to be the state song. Governor William T. Cahill never signed the bill into law, though, and despite much lobbying over the years, the song remains an unofficial anthem. In 2014, as schoolkids and others wrote to Governor Chris Christie to give the song an official title, a Teaneck filmmaker also launched a Kickstarter campaign to make a documentary about Mascara, his song, and their long and winding journey toward greatness. And so the saga continues…

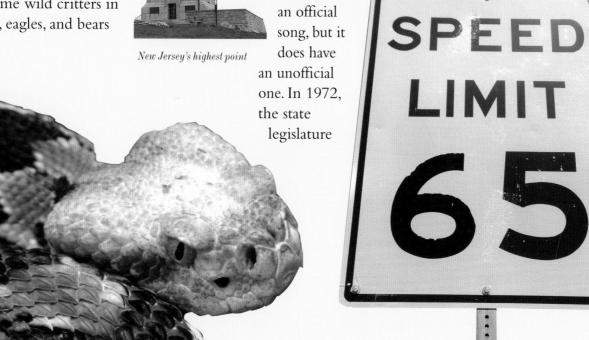

*The timber rattlesnake is one of two poisonous snakes found in New Jersey.*

**Did you know?**

New Jersey's weather predictor is a coatimundi named Terreto who lives at the Cohanzick Zoo in Bridgeton. Every Groundhog Day, Terreto looks for his shadow to predict when spring will come. The zoo's director swears this Central American relative of raccoons is more accurate than groundhogs.

*New Jerseyans have lobbied to get "I'm from New Jersey" to be their state song for more than 40 years.*

# The Jersey Devil

*You won't see Sasquatch or a chupacabra, and there's no Loch Ness. But if you're unlucky (er, lucky?), you might catch a glimpse of the Jersey Devil.*

*A 1919 article in a Philadelphia newspaper warns of a Jersey Devil sighting.*

## Once Upon a Time

Sometimes called the Flying Death, Jabberwok, Kingowing, Woozlebug, or Phantom of the Pines—the Jersey Devil occupies a mysterious but important place in the state's culture. Travelers to the Pine Barrens—a vast, dense wilderness of pine trees and oak forests in South Jersey—should be careful because they just might encounter this most enduring, scary, and elusive of all Jersey legends.

Tracking down the Jersey Devil can be a challenge, but tracking down its exact origins is almost impossible. The most popular version of the story begins on a dark and stormy night in 1735 when a woman named Mother Leeds went into labor in her cabin somewhere in

the Pine Barrens. A mother of 12 already, when she found she was pregnant yet again, Mother Leeds cried, "Let this one be a devil!" And so it was. Her "lucky" 13th child appeared healthy…at first. But then, before the eyes of the terrified midwives, he transformed into a hideous beast, sprouted wings, and flew up the chimney.

There are other origin stories: Some say the Devil devoured its mother. Others claim that Mother Leeds abandoned the healthy boy in the forest, where he transformed into a hideous monster. Some even place the origin of the Devil in 1778, when a young girl from Leeds Point fell in love with a British soldier; in that story, the Jersey Devil was the offspring of the treasonous union.

Sources are just as unclear as to where exactly the monster was

born. If you had passed through the Pine Barrens before the 1950s, the locals might have shown you the Shourds house in Leeds Point. This shack is no longer standing, but it was one supposed birthplace. Other Devil hunters might have pointed you to South Main Street in Pleasantville, or Estellville, or Mullica River. All of these places claim to have spawned the Jersey Devil.

Of course, if you truly want to find the Jersey Devil, it might help to know what it looks like. Unfortunately, no two witnesses have ever agreed on its appearance. The general consensus is that the Jersey Devil has the body of a kangaroo, the head of a horse, antlers, a forked reptilian tail, a man's torso, a goat's legs and hooves, and giant leathery wings—if you can picture that.

## The Devil's Territory

Throughout the 18th and 19th centuries, the Jersey Devil was blamed for all manner of misfortunes in the Pine Barrens. Wherever livestock died or crops refused to

*The densely wooded Pine Barrens are said to be the home of the terrifying Jersey Devil.*

grow was considered the Devil's territory. Parents used the legend to discipline their children, and locals used it to keep intruders out of the Pine Barrens.

In 1909, however, the legend became much more than folklore. Between January 16 and January 23, the Jersey Devil was supposedly spotted all over the Delaware River Valley. From South Jersey, the Devil zigzagged up through Camden and Philadelphia, Pennsylvania, leaving its hoofprints everywhere. People were scared. Witnesses claimed the Devil attacked a trolley car and was, in turn, fired upon by police but escaped. Later, William Wasso of Clayton claimed to have seen the creature's demise. As he watched, Wasso said, the Jersey Devil trailed its tail over the third rail of an electric railway and exploded in a ball of fire.

Still, the sightings continued, and New Jersey's citizens were so terrified of the creature that many refused to leave their homes—even in daylight. Mills in the Pine Barrens closed. In the town of Mount Ephraim, school was canceled—the state's first (and last) closing for supernatural causes. At the end of the week, though, without explanation, the sightings stopped and the hoofprints disappeared. There have never again been so many sightings in such a short

*One artist's rendering of the Jersey Devil shows a frightening beast.*

*Artist Jason McKittrick created this Jersey Devil "skull" for an exhibit at the Paranormal Museum in Asbury Park.*

time frame, much to the disappointment of Devil hunters everywhere.

## Devil Impersonators

Of course, such a panic provided ample opportunity for hucksters and hoaxers to cash in. G. W. Green of Salem admitted decades later that he made lots of money by selling phony photos, but he wasn't the only one. Smelling profit, others jumped on the Jersey Devil bandwagon. The Philadelphia Zoo announced an award of $10,000—a hefty sum in 1909—to anyone who could deliver the creature live to the zoo. It would doubtless be a popular exhibit, the zoo's superintendent reasoned.

Jacob F. Hope, an animal trainer, and Norman Jefferies, a publicist, managed to answer the zoo's call. The men announced that they had just recently had a creature in their possession that matched the Devil's description. This beast had escaped right before the many sightings, however, so they offered a reward of $500 for its capture.

Jefferies then got a kangaroo and brought it to Philadelphia. Once there, he painted it

green. The poor kangaroo almost died after it licked off the poisonous paint, so Jefferies repainted it (this time with less toxic paint). Then he attached large fake wings…which the kangaroo quickly destroyed. Jefferies attached a second, sturdier set, made of a bronze frame covered with rabbit fur, and ta-da! Having created an acceptable-looking Jersey Devil, Jefferies gathered up a team of locals, set the "creature" loose in Fairmount Park, and made a big show of capturing it again. Afterward the creature was put on display at the zoo in a cage with gnawed bones on the floor. Viewers were allowed to look at it for only one second each so as not to…ahem…spark its temper.

## Speak of the Devil

Sightings have mostly died down since then, but during the last couple of decades, the Jersey Devil has been honored in an episode of *The X-Files,* a B horror movie, and a video game (in which it hunts down radioactive carrots). The beast also lends its name to a drink in many South Jersey bars. So you may not spot the beast mauling cattle anymore, but it is alive and well—at least in the minds of New Jerseyans.

# The Blue and the Buff

*There's so much to learn from New Jersey's state flag.*

Washington selected this color scheme in 1780 for the uniforms of New Jersey's regiments during the War for Independence. Soldiers had to carry a state flag that matched their uniforms, and New Jersey's colors have been the same ever since. The traditional flag was made official in 1896.

*The Netherlands insignia inspired the New Jersey State flag.*

## The Blue

• The blue-hued part of the flag features the state's seal: two women flanking a shield crowned by a knight's helmet with a horse's head on top. Underneath this is a banner that reads "Liberty and Prosperity, 1776" and features the state motto along with the year of independence from Great Britain.

• The two women represent Liberty and Prosperity. "Liberty" holds a staff topped with a funny-looking hat called a Phrygian helmet, or a liberty cap. "Prosperity" has a proper name, Ceres, and is the Roman goddess of the harvest and agriculture. Her overflowing cornucopia represents all the good Jersey fresh produce.

• The three plows on the shield reemphasize the importance of agriculture to the state.

• The knight's helmet is a traditional European sign of state sovereignty and independence; the horse's head stands for strength and speed.

• No one seems to know for sure

## The Buff

Why a yellow background and blue shield? Because none other than General George Washington picked them out in 1779. The colors—Jersey blue and buff (as the yellow is called)—honor the Dutch, New Jersey's original European settlers. The colors first appeared on the insignia of the Netherlands, and

*George Washington meets with New Jersey soldiers at the Battle of Trenton.*

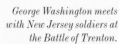

who designed the state seal: Some argue that Pierre Eugene du Simitiere, designer of the United States seal, was the artist. Others claim that Francis Hopkinson, a signer of the Declaration of Independence and designer of the first American flag, put it together.

*A second-century Greek bust shows a Phrygian helmet.*

*Ceres, the Roman goddess of agriculture, was the inspiration for Prosperity.*

# Kevin Smith Films: Five Fun Facts

1. *Clerks* (1994) was so full of profanity that it initially got an NC-17 rating based on language alone—the first film to achieve that distinction. Miramax, the film's distributor, hired celebrity lawyer Alan Dershowitz to appeal the rating. It worked; the film was rated R.

2. The two main characters in *Mallrats* (1995) were named T. S. Quint and Brodie Bruce—an homage to three of the main characters in *Jaws*: salty sea dog Quint, heroic police captain Brodie, and the mechanical shark (called Bruce) on the *Jaws* set.

3. Miramax offered Smith a $3 million budget for *Chasing Amy* (1997) if he made it with people with "star power." (At the time, the studio suggested Jon Stewart, David Schwimmer, and Drew Barrymore.) Smith made the film with the actors he preferred—for just $250,000. The movie made more than $12 million at the box office.

4. Because of its satirical look at religion, the 1999 film *Dogma* came under fire from many groups critical of its content. Smith infiltrated one of those groups and protested the film himself—he was even interviewed by a TV reporter while incognito.

5. Gay and lesbian groups protested *Jay and Silent Bob Strike Back* (2001) because of Jay's incessant homophobic comments, prompting Smith to put a disclaimer on the film that said: "I'm not sorry, because I didn't make the jokes at the expense of the gay community. I made jokes at the expense of two characters who neither I nor the audience have ever held up to be paragons of intellect. They're idiots."

# Classic Crank Calls

*Before caller ID, making crank phone calls was something of an adolescent rite of passage. But two bored guys from Jersey City elevated the practice into an art form.*

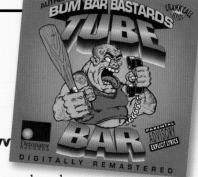

### The Granddaddy of All Prank Calls

It was the early 1970s, and John Elmo and Jim Davidson spent their free time making crank telephone calls and having fun at someone else's expense. These guys were true innovators: Instead of the tried and true "running refrigerator" and "Prince Albert in a can" gags, they would call business establishments—usually bars and taverns—and ask to have someone paged.

Of course, when the false first and last names were spoken together, they formed a humorous phrase. Hearing someone call out for Sal Lami or Cole Cutz provided endless hours of amusement.

One day, Davidson remembered a bar that he passed each day on his way to school and decided it would be the next target. When he called the Tube Bar in Jersey City and owner Louis "Red" Deutsch answered, Deutsch's raspy voice struck him as so funny that he never got around to making the joke. He just cracked up and hung up the phone. That call led him and Elmo on a yearlong practice of calling the bar just to hear Deutsch's voice and get a rise out of him.

Elmo and Davidson couldn't believe their luck when they called Red and heard him page "Phil Mypockets," "Pepe Roni," or "Al Coholic." Once Red

## "Paging Al Coholic"

Deutsch figured out that the callers were having some fun at his expense, he would become enraged and let loose a torrential outpouring of obscenities that would make the saltiest of sailors blush. Then he'd threaten the callers with extreme bodily harm if he ever got his hands on them.

### Seeing Red

Red himself was a larger-than-life character. At 6' 2" tall and weighing more than 200 pounds, he had become a regular fixture of Journal Square, the hub of downtown Jersey City. The square stood at the crossroads of several rail lines, so there was always a lot of pedestrian traffic. Beginning in the 1930s, Red had run a fruit and vegetable stand there, and everyone seemed to know him.

When Prohibition was repealed in 1933, Red opened a tavern in Journal Square. He named his establishment the Tube Bar, in recognition of the city's underground tubes (better known now as tunnels). The bar quickly became a success, and the colorful proprietor became something of a celebrity. Still, Red ran his bar with an iron fist. In his tavern, the customer was seldom right, and patrons had better heed the "boss" and abide by his rules…or else.

*Left: Louis "Red" Deutsch in the 1950s.*

*Red Deutsch ran the Tube Bar in Jersey City.*

## Paging Rufus Leakin

Red Deutsch didn't take guff from anyone, especially not a couple of punk kids on the telephone. When the prank calls began, he quickly learned to recognize his tormentors' voices. He would immediately go on the offensive, spewing out threats about what he would do to them when he got his hands on them (slicing open their bellies was a favorite). He also cast aspersions on their lives and habits. But the more enraged Red got, the funnier he became to the two callers.

Meanwhile, the personality of Journal Square was changing. A new underground transit depot opened in the 1970s, and pedestrian traffic dropped off. Red sold the bar in 1980 and moved to Palm Springs, Florida (where he died a few years later). But his rants were about to take on a life of their own.

*Reel-to-reel tapes like this one brought Red Deutsch's rants to the world.*

## And the Tape Rolls On

Elmo and Davidson had the foresight to record their prank calls to the Tube Bar and their heated conversations with Red Deutsch on big reel-to-reel tapes. When they entertained friends with the tapes, everyone asked for copies. Soon those friends made copies for their friends, who made copies for their friends, who made copies for…you get the idea. Soon the tapes were all over the country.

A manager for the New York Mets heard the tapes and played them for the team. The players enjoyed them so much that they played them for their friends on other teams, and soon all the major leaguers had heard them. The L.A. Dodgers had Tube Bar T-shirts printed, and the Miami Dolphins football team was rumored to play the tapes at practices. Still, no one knew who the tapes' authors were.

## D'oh, but No Dough

Because the tapes' originators remained anonymous, they received no compensation. At first, the tapes were passed from person to person. But soon some people along the way saw an opportunity to make money. Bootlegged versions of the tapes surfaced for sale.

Eventually Elmo and Davidson got tired of seeing others profit from their work. In 1993 they copyrighted their recordings. Calling themselves the Bar Bum Bastards (a term coined by another bartender they loved to annoy), they released *The Tube Bar* tapes under the Detonator label.

One more thing: If this story sounds familiar, it may be because TV's *The Simpsons* had a running gag that honors the Tube Bar tapes. Bart Simpson calls Moe, the bartender at Moe's Tavern, with requests to page a false customer. When Moe, whose gravelly voice sounds an awful lot like Red Deutsch, realizes that he's the victim of a prank, he lets loose a string of invective and threats to Bart's delight. There seems little doubt that the bit is an homage to the iconic New Jersey bar, its legendary owner, and the two crank callers.

*Moe growls at a prank caller on an episode of* The Simpsons.

# The Boss Sings About NJ

*Bruce Springsteen is as close to a songwriter laureate as New Jersey has ever had. Here is a sampling of his most geographically pertinent tunes.*

*Left: The colorful lights of Atlantic City brighten up the boardwalk.*

player, David Sancious, lived. Springsteen named the band for the street because he thought it sounded catchy. Sancious, however, left the band after this album.

## "Atlantic City"

**Album:** *Nebraska* (1982)
Atlantic City, of course, is New Jersey's famous gambling mecca, where the casinos exist somewhat uneasily with the city. The song is filled with references to gambling and also the mob: the Chicken Man who blows up in the first line of the song is a reference to a Philly-based mobster named Phil Testa, who was killed in mob warfare over control of Atlantic City.

## "The E Street Shuffle"

**Album:** *The Wild, the Innocent & the E Street Shuffle* (1973)
E Street—referenced in the song title, the album title, and the name of Springsteen's backing band—is the street in Belmar where the mother of Springsteen's then–piano

*Right: A sculpture of Springsteen's guitar marks the intersection of 10th Avenue and E Street in Belmar.*

## "4th of July, Asbury Park (Sandy)"

**Album:** *The Wild, the Innocent & the E Street Shuffle* (1973)

Asbury Park is a seaside resort town that has seen better days. Its fall from greatness inspired Springsteen and gave birth to some fantastic lyrics, including this bittersweet tribute to the Asbury Park boardwalk. The woman mentioned in the song is Madam Marie Castello, a fortune-teller who plied her trade there in the Temple of Knowledge. She took a brief hiatus, but then returned to her career in foresight until her death in 2008. (The Temple of Knowledge is still there, though, and her granddaughter reads the fortunes now.) The town itself has been making a comeback as well, with a new wooden boardwalk, new shops and restaurants, and a revitalization of its oceanfront neighborhoods.

*Above: Madam Marie began reading fortunes on the Asbury Park boardwalk in the 1930s.*

*A. A. Zimmerman circa 1895, a year after he turned professional.*

## "Tenth Avenue Freeze-out"

**Album:** *Born to Run* (1975)

Tenth Avenue, like E Street, runs through Belmar. This song refers to the band, with saxophonist Clarence Clemons making an appearance as the Big Man and Springsteen as Scooter.

## "In Freehold"

**Album:** Unreleased. The song made its first appearance at a 1996 concert in Freehold. This is Springsteen's shout-out to his hometown, whose biggest claims to fame are being the home of the Boss and of Arthur Augustus Zimmerman, who won the first bicycling sprint world championship in 1893.

*Springsteen lived in this house in Freehold as a child.*

# Ivy League Antics, Part I

*If undergraduates get wasted and do something stupid, it's a "mistake." But if they do it again the next year, it's a "tradition." And for Princeton University, which has been around since 1746, that's a lot of traditions.*

*Princeton's Big Cannon pokes out of the gravel on Cannon Green.*

## A Tale of Two Cannons

If you're strolling across Cannon Green on the Princeton campus, you may notice a strange black nub poking out of a ring of gravel. Across a path from the green is another black nub. Incredibly, these are both Revolutionary War cannons, buried nose-down in the ground.

Princeton was the site of a major battle during the Revolutionary War, and when the fighting ended, a few cannons were left lying around on campus. During the War of 1812, the Big Cannon, now in the middle of Cannon Green, was taken to New Brunswick, New Jersey. In 1835 Princeton locals stole it back…or at least tried to. They ended up dumping it on the side of the road

when their wagon broke. Four years later, Princeton students hauled it the rest of the way and planted it nose-down behind Nassau Hall to make sure it remained in town.

In 1875 some Rutgers students decided to steal back the cannon they thought belonged to them. Unfortunately, they cannon-napped the wrong one—they took the Little Cannon, which had never been to New Brunswick. As a result, the War of the Cannons was on. Princetonians planned to steal the gun back, but Rutgers students kept watch and cagily moved the Little Cannon from location to location. Princetonians then managed to steal some Revolutionary War muskets in their raid, as hostages for the Little Cannon. The heads of both schools finally negotiated a truce, and the cannon and muskets were returned to their rightful owners. The Little Cannon was planted on the Princeton campus as well, to prevent further raids. Rutgers still paints the Little Cannon red a few times a year, though, splashing "R.U." on the lawn around it, to remind Princeton that the war is not over.

## Clapper Capers

Another Princeton tradition has its roots in the grand old practice of cutting classes. In the 1860s, the bell in the tower of Nassau Hall ruled campus life. It rang at the start of the day, at curfew, and at the beginning of each class. One winter's night in 1863, an enterprising undergraduate snuck up the tower and stole

*The empty bell tower of Nassau Hall*

*The bell from Nassau Hall is now on display at Princeton's First Campus Center.*

the bell's clapper. The next morning the bell couldn't ring—no bell, no classes. After that, it became a tradition for entering freshmen to steal the clapper. Members of the administration resigned themselves to the thefts and kept a barrel of extra clappers on hand. The tradition finally ended more than a century—and many injuries—later. In 1991 the university removed the clapper permanently. The bell continues to toll on the Princeton campus, though, as a mechanical striker was installed in 1955.

## Princeton's a Riot

In 1865 it was fashionable to carry walking canes, but Princeton's upperclassmen decided the freshmen should not be allowed to do it. The sophomores in particular decided to take these status symbols away from the freshmen. Sophomores waiting on Nassau Street one evening tried to grab the canes away from freshmen, resulting in a brawl. This was the first Cane Spree, a term that, at the time, meant a ruckus. Since then, every year the freshman and sophomore classes have faced off in the fall for the annual Cane Spree. The original rules? The Cane Spree took place at midnight on the night of the October full moon in front of one of the dorms. The contest, lit only by broom torches, started with three organized bouts between white-clad freshmen and black-clad sophomores. After that, an all-out rumpus broke out as underclassmen wrestled for each other's canes. In the late 1920s, a few new rules were added: no throwing of dangerous missiles and no "parading in the streets in an undressed condition" (that tradition would come

*Above and below: Upperclassmen go after freshmen during Cane Spree's glory days.*

later). Apparently firecrackers, rocks, and iron bedsteads were commonly thrown during previous brawls.

Over the years the Cane Spree has become more sedate. In 1951 football and track events were added. Women first participated in 1970. Nowadays, the Cane Spree is a set of organized athletic contests between the sophomore and freshman classes, with bragging rights going to the winners.

*For more Princeton traditions, turn to page 116.*

# Hometowns: Elizabeth

*What can you get for 20 fathoms of trading cloth, two coats, ten bars of lead, and assorted other sundries? The town of Elizabeth.*

*An old map shows Elizabeth in the 1600s.*

## The Stats

**Location:** Union County

**Founded:** 1665

**Current Population:** 126,458 (2012)

**Size:** 11.69 square miles. Originally the township encompassed all of Union County. It shrank to its current size as 12 towns broke away over the years.

**What's in a Name?** You may think it was named for Queen Elizabeth I, but it wasn't. Elizabethtown ("town" was dropped from the name in 1740 when King George II granted its charter) was named for another Englishwoman who never set foot in North America—Elizabeth Carteret, wife of the coproprietor of East Jersey, Sir George Carteret. (Her husband never set foot in New Jersey either.)

## Claims to Fame

- In 1664 the Native Americans of Staten Island sold the land where Elizabeth now stands for "20 fathoms of trading cloth, two coats, two guns, ten bars of lead, two kettles, two handfuls of gunpowder, and 400 fathoms of white wampum."

- Elizabeth has the largest seaport in the United States.

- The Elizabeth Marine Terminal was the world's first port designed specifically to handle standardized containers. Exit 13A on the Turnpike was built to give trucks direct access to the containerport.

- Elizabeth is home to Jersey Gardens, the largest outlet mall in the state.

*Elizabeth Station (left) connects residents to New York. The city's port (below) is the largest in the United States.*

# Jersey's Jaws

*In a world of innocence, in a time of war, man faces an ancient struggle: just when you thought it was safe to go in the water...shark attack!*

## Beach Haven or Hell?

Before July 1916, most educated Americans didn't believe in man-eating sharks. They thought old sailors' tales about the animals were no more real than those about the kraken or sea serpents. But five attacks, four deaths, and one mean shark at the Jersey Shore proved all the scientists wrong.

That fateful summer, Charles Vansant, a recent college grad from Philadelphia, was escaping the sweltering city heat with his family at Beach Haven, a resort on the Jersey Shore. In the late afternoon of July 1, 1916, Vansant decided to go swimming and dove into the waves.

That's when beachgoers spotted a lone fin heading straight for him. They yelled, "Watch out! Watch out!" but he couldn't hear them. Although Vansant was less than 50 feet from shore, in water just 3.5 feet deep, something slammed into him and closed its powerful jaws around his left leg.

Future Olympic swimmer Alexander Ott was also on the beach. He rushed into the bloody water to Vansant's aid, starting a tug-of-war with the predator. With the help of others from the crowd, Ott managed to drag Vansant onto the sand, but only a bloody stump remained where Vansant's left leg should have been. In modern times, these injuries would not necessarily have been fatal, but in 1916 Vansant's father, a doctor, had no idea how to treat his son. Charles Vansant died of blood loss shortly after the attack.

Despite the fact that Vansant's was the first death certificate in the United States to list "shark" as the cause of death, the hotel at Beach Haven didn't warn any other resorts of the potential threat. Most people didn't even believe it could have been a shark anyway— after all, they reasoned, sharks didn't eat people. When the attack *was* reported, it was buried on the last page of the *New York Times* three days later under the innocuous headline "Dies After Attack by Fish." So all along the Jersey Shore, vacationers continued their carefree aquatic recreation.

## For Whom the Bellboy Tolls

Five days after Vansant's death, Charles Bruder, the head bellboy at a hotel in Spring Lake (a resort about 50 miles north of Beach Haven), took a break from his duties and, like Vansant before him, went for a swim in the ocean. He was a quarter mile from the shore when observers saw a spray of water erupt around him. As rescuers hauled him into a boat, they saw that a shark had taken off both his legs and gouged his abdomen and chest. Bruder remained conscious until they reached shore, where he died before a doctor could reach him.

**SHARK SIGHTED TODAY**

**ENTER WATER AT OWN RISK**

*The July 7, 1916, edition of the* Evening Ledger *details New Jersey's valiant efforts to battle a man-eating shark.*

21

*Unsuspecting swimmers wade into the ocean on the Jersey Shore.*

The hotel manager at Spring Lake immediately put out the first coastwide shark alarm in the United States. After July 6, thousands of swimmers rushed back to dry land as a full-scale shark panic set in. Dozens of men headed out to sea in boats, aiming rifles into the waves to kill the murderous shark. Beaches set up nets around the shore, assuring swimmers that it was safe to swim within those confines.

There were still naysayers who believed the attacks were committed by a killer whale or giant sea turtle—some even said it must have been a swordfish. Most notably, Dr. Frederick Lucas, director of the American Museum of Natural History in New York, called the idea of a shark attack ridiculous, saying that a shark could not "nip off a man's leg like biting a carrot."

## Up the Creek Without a Paddle

In the early morning of July 12, and old sea captain named Thomas Cottrell saw a shark while on his morning walk. There was only one problem: He was in Matawan, 10 miles from the ocean. The shark he saw must have swum through Raritan Bay and up Matawan Creek, a freshwater creek only 17 feet at its deepest point. Cottrell rushed to town to sound the alarm—and was laughed at. A shark in the creek? Pshaw!

Meanwhile, six adolescent boys were enjoying a dip in the creek. Lester Stilwell floated on his back and called out, "Watch me float, fellas!" But when the fellas, mere yards away in the creek, turned to watch, they saw Lester floating...as the jaws of a shark surrounded him. The tail of the shark slammed one of the other boys into the pier as it claimed its prey.

The five survivors ran down the main street of Matawan screaming, "Shark! Shark!" In a matter of moments, a rescue team appeared, but they scoffed at the boys' tale. They simply thought Lester, whom everyone in town knew was prone to seizures, had lost control in the water and drowned.

## Who Rescues the Rescuers?

They trawled the creek for the body but had little success. Two men, Stanley Fisher and George Burlew, dove into the deepest part of the murky creek and tried to locate the boy's body in the muddy water. After a while, Fisher surfaced and cried, "I've got it!" He had found Lester's body...lodged in the jaws of a feeding shark. In a moment of startling stupidity, Fisher pried the body from the man-eater and made for the surface, but the shark struck him as he reached it. Fisher had to drop Lester's body in order to struggle to shore. Only as he was climbing out of the creek did he notice his left leg—and how little of it remained. The shark had taken a giant bite and stripped the leg from hip to knee.

Dr. Reynolds, the local general practitioner, thought the bite was poisonous and wouldn't touch it. The nearest hospital was 10 miles away, and Fisher died just before he got there, more than three hours later.

Hysteria kept spreading. Fishermen raced up and down the creek in boats, yelling at swimmers to get out of the water. But it was too late for a group of boys swimming just a quarter mile downstream from the site of the two previous attacks. As Joseph Dunn made for the ladder, he felt something hit him. He watched in horror as a shark turned around and grabbed his leg, trying to pull him into deeper water. Fortunately for Joseph, the water was so shallow that the shark couldn't maneuver. It let the boy go and swam away. Joseph's leg was mangled, but he survived.

## Never Mind the Germans

For the rest of that day, the citizens of Matawan hunted the killer shark. They set off dynamite in the creek; then, seeing the movement of bubbles caused by the dynamite, they fired their rifles, shouting, "Shark! Shark!" A doctor pointed out that the blood from all the fish killed by the dynamite might actually attract more sharks, but the shark hunters were undeterred.

Shark panic swept the New Jersey coast as fishermen killed dozens of sharks over the next weeks. Angry citizens wrote letters to President Woodrow Wilson demanding that he make their waters safe again. Some saw the shark as a dark companion of a German U-boat that had appeared on the coast at the same time. Wilson did meet with his cabinet on the subject, but decided that an all-out war on sharks wasn't in the U.S. government's budget.

## Shark: 4, Man: 1

John Murphy and Michael Schleisser launched their small motorboat into Raritan Bay on July 14 for some recreational fishing, trailing a net behind them. Their boat suddenly slammed to a halt: They had something *big* in their net, and it was pulling their boat backward and under the water. The catch turned out to be a shark that started chomping at the two men over the gunwales of the boat.

Schleisser grabbed a broken oar handle, the only weapon available, and managed to beat the shark to death.

Schleisser was also a renowned taxidermist, and he brought his prize home to stuff. When he opened the stomach he found what the Museum of Natural History confirmed were human bones. At the time, there was no way to match the bones with the victims for certain, but most believed the man-killer was gone for good.

## Expert Opinion

So what caused all the sudden shark attacks on Jersey's shore? The most common theory for many years was that the attacks were due to a single rogue shark. Scientists knew that individual lions or tigers can develop a taste for humans even though the animals don't generally go after human prey, so it seemed like a reasonable assumption for sharks as well. Modern shark experts dismiss the rogue shark theory, though. They suggest that cluster attacks, like the ones in 1916, can be the result of coastal water temperature changes that draw multiple sharks to the beaches.

However, the number of fatalities also had to do with the quality of medical attention at the time. Medical knowledge is more advanced now than it was in 1916, and as a result, more victims of shark attacks survive their encounters. But even so, sharks still sometimes make people afraid to go in the water, even in New Jersey.

*The July 1919 issue of the* Philadelphia Inquirer *tells New Jersey's deadly shark attack tale.*

# Trenton Makes, the World Takes

*Ever wonder where the slogan on Trenton's bridge comes from?*
*We did too. Here's the story.*

*An 1875 drawing shows the original Trenton Bridge.*

*John Roebling's wire-rope factory in Trenton (left) made the wire used to build the Brooklyn Bridge (above and below).*

## Golden Age

If you've driven through New Jersey, you probably know the slogan of its capital city: "Trenton Makes, the World Takes." It's hard to miss—spelled out in giant neon letters and emblazoned on the side of the Trenton-Morrisville Bridge. Nicknamed the Trenton Makes Bridge by locals, it runs parallel to the commuter train tracks, so thousands of passengers see it every day.

Where did the slogan come from? It turns out that in its heyday, Trenton was quite the manufacturing powerhouse.

Strategically located between New York City and Philadelphia on the Delaware River, Trenton was once a booming center of commerce and industry. Connected to the coalfields of Pennsylvania and the iron mines of New Jersey, the city became famous for its ironworks. John Roebling, a German immigrant, set up a wire-rope factory in Trenton in 1849. Roebling's company supplied wire for aqueducts and suspension bridges all over the country— and some nearby. Roebling also designed the Brooklyn Bridge…after getting incredibly annoyed that he had to wait a long time for a ferry. He convinced the State of New York to finance the bridge and also suggested the construction of the Williamsburg and Queensboro Bridges, which were later also built over the East River. In 1869 Roebling's foot was crushed while inspecting a tower site for the Brooklyn Bridge; he later died of tetanus from the injury.

His son Washington and later Washington's wife Emily took over construction of the Brooklyn Bridge, which is still held up with Roebling wire, made in Trenton.

By the middle of the 19th century, Trenton had become the nation's center of iron manufacture. Other industries also grew up in the city—in particular, it was the center of American ceramics manufacturing, creating $50 million worth of goods in 1910.

## Trenton Makes

So it's obvious why Trenton's city fathers chose the slogan "Trenton Makes, the World Takes" in 1910. It was picked out of 1,477 submissions in a contest held by the Trenton Chamber of Commerce. Future state senator S. Roy Heath came up with the slogan. His daughter, Dartha, described her dad as "one shrewd Quaker. He knew he could get ahead if he worked hard. That's why people came to this city, for the opportunity." In 1917 the sign was updated

with 2,400 electric bulbs—the largest slogan sign in the world at the time, according to the *Trenton Daily State Gazette*. The sign was replaced again in 1935—the new neon slogan stood 7 feet high and 330 feet long.

Sadly, over time, the sign became something of a joke. In the move to nationalize industries, Trenton suffered as one after another of its businesses left. John A. Roebling's Sons Company moved out in 1952, and it was official: Trenton didn't make much of anything anymore.

## The World Takes

The sign is still there. It went dark in 1973 due to the oil crisis, and the city couldn't afford the electric bills. Local businesses paid to have it replaced in 1980. In 2004 a local newspaper suggested that the bridge be updated with a new, different slogan. Trentonians were outraged and wrote hundreds of angry letters. Mayor

*From teacups to toilets: Trenton started producing pottery in the mid-19th century.*

Douglas Palmer vowed to fight any efforts to change the beloved sign. After seeing how much the Trenton Makes sign was loved, the Delaware River Joint Toll Bridge Commission, the agency that owned the bridge, decided not to change the slogan at all. But they did freshen it up in 2005. It blazes on today.

*The famous slogan lights up the Trenton–Morrisville Bridge.*

# New Jersey Notables

*Not content to specialize, New Jersey has produced some of the finest artists, scholars, heroes, and athletes the world has ever known. Here are some of the finest.*

## Alfred Stieglitz

Born in 1864 in Hoboken, this pioneering photographer fought to put photography on the same artistic level as painting. His photographs were the first accepted as art by major museums in Boston, New York City, and Washington, D.C. He married artist Georgia O'Keeffe in 1924, and some of his most famous photographs are of her.

*Alfred Stieglitz*

## Charles Addams

Born in Westfield in 1912, this famous cartoonist created a pop-culture phenomenon and beloved TV show (*The Addams Family*) inspired by his fascination with humor and the macabre. He won both a Mystery Writers of America Award and the Yale Humor Award.

## Queen Latifah

Born Dana Owens in 1970 in Newark, Queen Latifah (whose name means "delicate" and "sensitive" in Arabic) was the first female rapper to have an album go gold—her third release, *Black Reign*. Her biggest single "U.N.I.T.Y." won a Grammy that year for Best Solo Rap Performance. Not limiting herself to music, she has also excelled in acting and was nominated for an Academy Award in 2003.

## Dorothea Lange

Another photographer from Hoboken, Lange was born in 1895 and is best known for documenting the destitute conditions of migrant workers who traveled to California during the Great Depression. She was the first woman awarded a Guggenheim Fellowship for photography.

## Lauryn Hill

A native of South Orange, Lauryn Hill first became well known as a member of the Fugees, whose album *The Score* became one of the highest-selling rap albums of all time. Blending many musical styles, her 1998 solo effort won five Grammys: Album of the Year, Best New Artist, Best Female R&B Vocal Performance, Best R&B Song, and Best R&B Album.

*Lauryn Hill performs in 2014.*

## Ruth St. Denis

A modern dancer extraordinaire, this Newark native born in 1879 left a major impact on ballet and modern dance. As a dancer and choreographer, St. Denis was greatly influenced by Asian and Anglo-European culture and was fascinated by exotic dance steps and costumes.

## Patricia McBride

A famous ballerina born in Teaneck in 1942, McBride joined the New York City Ballet in 1959, and by 1961 had become its youngest principal dancer. During her career, she worked with some of ballet's greats: George Balanchine, Jerome Robbins, Rudolf Nureyev, and Mikhail Baryshnikov.

*Dorothea Lange (shown here in 1936) photographed Depression-era migrant workers for the U.S. government.*

## Molly Pitcher

General George Washington commemorated this Trenton-born revolutionary for her heroic role at the Battle of Monmouth. The battle was fought on a hot June day, and Molly Pitcher hauled water to the battlefront for the men. When one soldier fell, she took his place at the cannon and kept it firing.

*Molly Pitcher loads a cannon.*

## H. Norman Schwarzkopf Jr.

Born in Trenton in 1934, Schwarzkopf graduated from the U.S. Military Academy at West Point. He is best known for his success as the commander of Operations of Desert Shield and Desert Storm during the first Gulf War.

## William J. Brennan Jr.

A Newark native, William J. Brennan Jr. believed the Constitution to be "a sparkling vision of the supreme dignity of every individual." President Dwight D. Eisenhower nominated him to become a Supreme Court justice in 1956, and he's considered one of the most influential justices in American history.

## Antonin Scalia

Born in Trenton in 1936, Scalia was nominated to the Supreme Court by President Ronald Reagan in 1986 and, as of 2014, was the longest-serving justice on the court. He's considered one of the most consistently conservative justices and is known for his acerbic wit, once saying, "A law can be both economic folly and constitutional."

## Grover Cleveland

This 22nd and 24th president of the United States was born in Caldwell in 1837. Although he took many unpopular stands during his political career—most notably, he ordered in the U.S. Army to stop strikers during the 1894 Pullman Strike, ensuring that the nation's railroads kept running—he's also considered one of the country's most honorable presidents and became the first, and as yet only, commander in chief to get married in the White House.

## Donna Weinbrecht

Moguls freestyle skiing was a pretty new event when Donna Weinbrecht from West Milford, New Jersey, became the first American to medal in it at the 1992 Olympic Games.

## Joe Theismann

Born in 1949, this All-American quarterback grew up in South River,

*Donna Weinbrecht leaps for the gold at the 1992 Olympics.*

graduated from Notre Dame University in 1970, and went on to total 25,206 yards passing with the Washington Redskins. He led his team to victory in Super Bowl XVII (1983) and was voted into the New Jersey Sports Hall of Fame.

## Franco Harris

Born in 1950 and another inductee into the New Jersey Sports Hall of Fame, this Fort Dix native is probably best known for his famous catch—the "Immaculate Reception"—where he caught a ball dropped by teammate John Fuqua and ran it in for a touchdown, leading the Pittsburgh Steelers to a 13–7 playoff victory over the Oakland Raiders in 1972. Over his career, he rushed for 1,000 yards in a season eight times, won four Super Bowls, and was selected the Most Valuable Player of Super Bowl IX (1975).

# Count Basie: Red Bank's Royalty

*There was no hotter jazz musician in the 1930s than William "Count" Basie. And even though he's often associated with Kansas City jazz, this music giant actually hailed from Red Bank.*

### He Really Wanted to Play Drums

As a child, Basie's first instrument wasn't the piano but the drums. He played the skins with his school band, but when it turned out that another kid was better, Basie got discouraged and quit the instrument. Fortunately for him, his mother was an enthusiastic amateur pianist and encouraged him to take that up. The piano suited Basie well, and by 1924, at the age of 20, he'd headed to Harlem to learn at the knee of legendary jazz pianist Fats Waller, who then recommended him to a traveling vaudeville show. In 1927 that vaudeville tour ended, and Basie found himself in Kansas City, where he stuck around playing piano until 1936. Then he and his orchestra headed for New York and national fame. (Incidentally, the kid who played drums better than Basie was a guy named Sonny Greer, who went on to spend three decades playing with Duke Ellington.)

*Basie and his orchestra appeared in the 1974 film Blazing Saddles.*

### He Wasn't Really a Count

Basie was the son of a coachman and a laundress, humble beginnings for jazz royalty. But the reason he's known as "Count" Basie dates back to the 1930s, when he formed a band from the remnants of two earlier bands and performed with the group on a Kansas City shortwave radio station. The radio announcer, riffing off the royalty names of jazz great Duke Ellington, dubbed Basie a count. The nickname stuck, but Basie was also known as the Jump King in Kansas City, because of his band's relentless rhythm.

*Count Basie tickles the ivories in the 1940s.*

## He Got Ripped Off for His Earliest Recordings

Musicians in modern times tend to complain about the rapacious nature of the music industry. But today's music companies have nothing on the sheer effrontery of the music industry in the 1930s. Basie's first recording contract is a fine example of how musicians got manhandled: In exchange for 24 "sides" (this was in the days of 78-rpm records, so one "side" equaled one song) over three years, Basie got a mere $750. Royalties? Forget about it. This is why Basie never made much money from early hits like "One o'Clock Jump" or "Jumpin' at the Woodside."

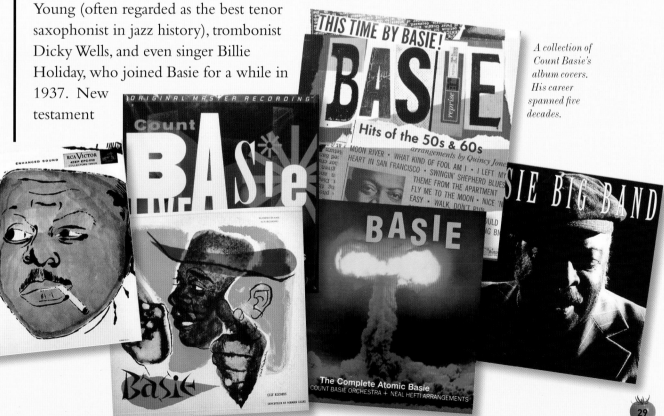

Count Basie (at the piano) performs with jazz singer Billie Holiday (right) in a 1951 film.

## His Musical Career Is Divided up into "Testaments"

Basie's career has an old testament (prior to 1950) and a new testament (everything after 1952). The dividing line falls during that two-year gap when the bottom seemed to drop out for swing and jazz orchestras. For economic reasons, in 1950 Basie had to drop his full orchestra and continue with just an eight-piece band. In 1952 things picked up again, and Basie was able to hire a full orchestra.

On either side of this gap, Basie's orchestras were substantially different. His old

testament musicians relied on memorizing arrangements (these were called "head arrangements" because the changes and parts were stored in the musicians' memories) rather than reading music. The new testament orchestras, on the other hand, were filled with sight readers (players who not only read music, but read it well enough to play it right away), which gave Basie more flexibility with his arrangements.

Which testament is better? That's a personal choice, of course. Both, however, were known for their excellent musicians. Old testament musicians included Lester Young (often regarded as the best tenor saxophonist in jazz history), trombonist Dicky Wells, and even singer Billie Holiday, who joined Basie for a while in 1937. New testament

standouts included saxophonist Eddie "Lockjaw" Davis, trumpeter Clark Terry, and vocalist Joe Williams.

## The Count Remembered His Roots

Despite the fact that Count Basie is almost always associated with Kansas City, he never forgot his hometown; one of the best-known numbers from his *Atomic Mr. Basie* album (1957) is "The Kid from Red Bank." And Red Bank has repaid Basie's compliment and honored his memory. In 1984, the year Basie passed away, the city renamed its Monmouth Arts Center the Count Basie Theater. In 2004 the city's annual Red Bank Jazz and Blues Festival (now called the Jersey Shore Jazz and Blues Festival), which draws more than 150,000 music lovers annually, celebrated the centennial of Basie's birth.

*A collection of Count Basie's album covers. His career spanned five decades.*

# It's the Law!

*Think you're a law-abiding citizen of New Jersey? Think again!*
*You may be breaking the law without even knowing it!*

## Behind the Wheel

- Need some shut-eye? Then don't even think about getting behind the wheel: New Jersey's made it a crime to drive while tired.

- If you need another reason not to drive after having a few drinks, a DUI conviction in New Jersey means you may never again apply for personalized license plates.

*Want a personalized New Jersey license plate? Don't drink and drive.*

## Fashion Police

- Don't wear anything on your head or in your hair in the streets of Secaucus that can accidentally (or purposely!) cut another person.

- For that matter, avoid wearing hat pins (with or without hats) throughout the state: It is illegal to wear them in public.

- Don't cross-dress in Haddon Township: men may not wear skirts in public.

*Right: This woman would be in violation of the law in Seacaucus.*

## Keep It Clean

- In Blairstown, keep your oaks to yourself. No street-side trees are allowed, lest they "obscure the air."

- Garden at will in Cranford, but keep your boat off the lawn. No aquatic vehicle parking is allowed.

- Smoke 'em if you've got 'em—but don't drop the ashes on the sidewalks of Blairstown. It is illegal to dirty the walkways with tobacco by-products.

- You may not dig for uranium in Jefferson Township, no matter how rich it might make you; you can't carry uranium around in your pockets, either.

## Animal Behavior

- In Cresskill, cats have to announce their presence properly by wearing three bells to warn nearby birds of their imminent arrival.

- Felines and humans alike should steer clear of homing pigeons. It is illegal to delay or detain one anywhere in the state.

- In Essex Fells, it is illegal for ducks to quack after 10:00 p.m.

# The Name Game

The band Fountains of Wayne named itself after a local fountain-and-lawn decor store on Route 46 in the town of Wayne, New Jersey. The shop closed in 2009, but during its glory days, patrons could find cement birdbaths, faux Roman statues, garden benches, and other decorations for the lawn. Fountains of Wayne (the store) is probably best known for its annual, ornate, animated Christmas displays. People came from all over to see the Christmas Emporium, made up of animatronic figures and multiple Santas in myriad scenes, like Christmas in Venice, Santa at the Shore, and Santa in the Rain Forest. (Fountains of Wayne, the band, is best known for its 2003 single "Stacy's Mom.")

*Above: A person feeds a homing pigeon. It's illegal to detain these animals anywhere in New Jersey.*

## Mind Your Manners

• Throughout the state, you better not slurp your soup. Audible eating could result in a citation.

• Be nice to law enforcement, because it is against the law across the state to frown at police officers—even when they're writing you a ticket.

*Kids, don't slurp your soup in New Jersey.*

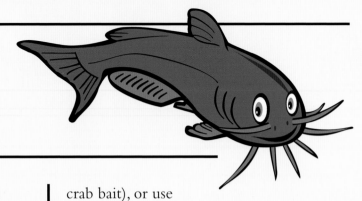

# Gone Fishing

*Sure, it may be called the Garden State, but New Jersey could just as easily be the Fishing State. Here are a few of our most savory swimmers.*

## American Shad

Also known as "poor man's salmon," these giant herrings abound in the Delaware River and spawn for their annual run from the end of March through June. Some of the juiciest spots include Byram, Lambertville, Bulls Island Recreation Area, and anywhere in the Delaware Water Gap Recreational Area. Here's the trick: Watch the Delaware's depth. If it's higher than normal, fish from the shore, casting a shad dart upstream and letting it bounce around the bottom. If the water level is normal or low, fishing from a boat is your best bet.

## Bass

Largemouth, smallmouth, and striped bass make up most of the state's bass action. New Jersey stripers became so popular in the 1970s and '80s that the population was in danger (swift wildlife management restored them).

Fish for largemouth in early spring and summer; stripers come into freshwater tidal flats to spawn only in the summer, whereas smallmouths can be caught all year long. Look for stripers in the Delaware River and Delaware Bay.

## Blue Crabs

Maryland certainly boasts about its blue crabs, but New Jersey has plenty of them too, all along the state's tidal waters, especially in shallow bays. Lure them on baited string lines and net them as they get close (not-so-fresh chicken or fish heads make good blue

*Left: The state's striped bass were so overfished in the 1970s and '80s that the federal government had to step in to save them.*

*New Jersey has many good spots for catching blue crabs.*

crab bait), or use a cage trap, for sale at local sporting goods stores. If you catch a blue crab with red claws and a brightly colored sponge on the bottom, however, throw it back. That's an expectant mother, and catching those is not just ungentlemanly—it's illegal. The crabs are ripe for the picking May through December.

## Bluefish

Saltwater bluefish can grow more than three feet long! You can catch adults by chumming (dumping oily, ground-up fish into the water) from a boat or by casting into the surf from the sand. Young ones, known as snappers, can be caught with small lures in bay areas. Bluefish are aggressive eaters and tend to strike at anything put in front of them. You'll find them from May to December. You'll also find them to be good eating. They're delicious when grilled whole with olive oil and garlic, and provide a big meal—a single fish can net around five pounds of meat.

## Catfish

And you thought catfish only swam in the South! It turns out that there are plenty of Yankee catfish, too, and some live in New Jersey. From the small brown bullhead variety to the larger white catfish and the revered channel catfish, summer is the best time to reel in these tasty vittles. The most prized New Jersey catfish is the channel catfish, which grows to trophy size and likes to come out at night. The best places to fish for them are on the bottom of the Delaware River and its many tidal tributaries. Fishing for catfish doesn't require any fancy equipment. A plain old worm on a hook will do.

## Fluke

Also known as summer flounder, this is the must-have fish on the Jersey coast. Experts say it's the most sought-after sport fish in the region from May through October. It's a saltwater fish, so you need to be coastal to catch one; but it can be caught either from a boat or from the shore. Using strips of squid and smaller baitfish, keep your bait in constant motion and drag it along the bottom.

## Marlin

At an average weight of about 100 pounds, this beautiful finned fish will give you both a healthy fight and enough meat for a large dinner party. Marlin live only in the Atlantic Ocean; both the white and blue varieties can be found off the Jersey coast in deep waters during the summer and early fall. Trolling and casting both work on these guys—use trolling baits or lures during the day and squid at night. Just be careful, because these fish can get pretty big: the record blue marlin catch in New Jersey waters weighed 1,046 pounds!

## Perch

These tasty catches are another New Jersey favorite, good for fishing all year round (even ice fishing!). These little fighters prefer the open water and travel in thick schools. You can find both yellow and white perch in New Jersey, and both species are easy to catch with a fish finder if you can come across a school. White perch are found in a number of the state's lakes, including

*Above: Marlins like this one can weigh hundreds of pounds.*

Greenwood, Hopatcong, Swartswood, Lenape, and Malaga. Look for white perch in the Delaware River and its lower tributaries, too.

*Ice fishing is just one of the ways to catch perch in the Garden State.*

# Big Booming Business

*It may not be the biggest state in the nation, but New Jersey is home to some pretty big businesses.*

### Let's Go to the Videotape

In New Jersey, there's a huge vault of more than 100 million feet of film—all of it footage of professional football. An obsessed fan's basement? Nope. We're talking about the official home of NFL Films, which has been in Mount Laurel for more than 50 years.

### I Am Stuck on Jersey, Cause Jersey's Stuck on Me

Just about everything in your bathroom can come from Johnson & Johnson, a leading manufacturer of health-care products. Making everything from Band-Aids to baby shampoo, Johnson & Johnson has made its home in New Brunswick since its founding in 1886. The company has grown to include 190 operating companies in 51 countries, with $27.5 billion in sales. That's a lot of boo-boos.

### The Rock of Ages

The financial behemoth Prudential Financial got its start in 1875 as the Prudential Friendly Society in downtown Newark, where its headquarters are still located today. The Pru has expanded from a business that provided life insurance for the working class to one of the largest financial service providers in the world.

### Gotta Getta Stuffed Animal

Need a teddy bear? How about a floppy stuffed dog? Look no further than Edison, where Gund's headquarters are. This stuffed toy manufacturer trademarked its "understuffing" methodology, which created the softest, most squishable toys suitable for repeated bouts of hugging.

*Below: Prudential's headquarters in 1956. The company is still there today.*

## A Blind Man's Best Friend

It's hard to remember a time when guide dogs weren't around. We have the Seeing Eye in Morristown to thank for that. It is North America's oldest guide dog–training institute. Located in New Jersey since 1931, the Seeing Eye was founded with the goal of helping blind people to live independently with the assistance of these specially trained dogs. More than 16,000 dogs have been placed with the blind since the school's founding.

## Tiny Bubbles

Every time a heavy package comes in the mail, what's inside is often protected with Bubble Wrap, another New Jersey innovation. In the 1950s, Marc A. Chavannes and Alfred W. Fielding were trying to develop textured wallpaper by capturing air between two thin layers of plastic. The wallpaper idea didn't take off, but the two realized that their invention was a perfect protective packing material. Bubble Wrap was born (and would become a favorite plaything for kids who couldn't get enough of popping those little plastic bubbles). In 1960 the two men founded the Sealed Air Corporation; the corporate headquarters are located in Elmwood Park, and the company still makes Bubble Wrap and other protective packaging gear today.

*Above: This statue of Seeing Eye founder Morris Frank and his dog Buddy greets visitors in downtown Morristown.*

# Jersey Bites

- Franklin Township is home to one of the first concrete highways in America. Thomas Edison's plant created the makings for this "Concrete Mile" in 1912.

- New Jersey isn't the only state where it's illegal to pump your own gas. It's also illegal in Oregon.

- When Meryl Streep placed her handprints in the sidewalk outside of Grauman's Chinese Theatre in Hollywood, someone asked her if, as a kid growing up in Summit, New Jersey, she thought that would ever happen. She quipped: "In New Jersey, we put other things in cement."

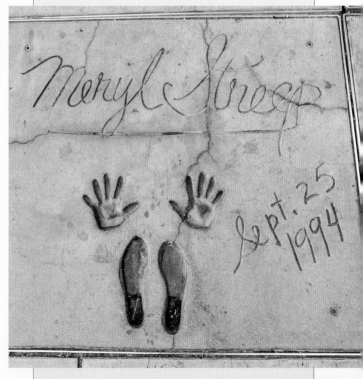

# Hometowns: Weehawken

*Along the banks of the Hudson River sits the town of Weehawken, a former dueling that is now a New Jersey legend.*

## The Stats

**Location:** Hudson County

**Founded:** Originally part of Hoboken, Weehawken broke off to become its own town in 1859.

**Population:** 12,521 (2012)

**Size:** 0.85 square mile

**What's in a Name?** Despite its sound, Weehawken does not refer to some kind of small predatory bird. The widely accepted derivation of the town's name is that it comes from the Algonquian word for "land of maize."

## Claims to Fame

- Weehawken is home to one end of the Lincoln Tunnel, the world's only "three-tube underwater vehicular tunnel facility," which opened in 1937. Today it's the busiest traffic tunnel in the world—an average of 120,000 cars pass through it daily.

- Weekhawken is the place where, on July 11, 1804, the sitting vice president of the United States, Aaron Burr, mortally wounded former secretary of the treasury Alexander Hamilton during their famous duel. Hamilton died the next day.

*Above and top: More than 100,000 cars travel through the Lincoln Tunnel every day.*

*Left: A drawing shows Aaron Burr shooting Alexander Hamilton during their 1804 duel.*

# Fun at the End of the Line

*Towering atop cliffs lining the Hudson River, the Palisades Amusement Park provided sizzling summer entertainment for three generations.*

## A Park by Any Other Name...

On Palisades Avenue in Cliffside Park, New Jersey, is the Little Park of Memories. Behind the bus stop, this park is literally paved with memories—underfoot are bricks bearing the happy remembrances of fans of the late, great Palisades Amusement Park, one of the first amusement parks ever built. Plaques and flags at this site celebrate the 74 years that the amusement park occupied the surrounding 38 acres and offered rides, games, shows, food, and fun to millions.

Originally called the Park on the Palisades, it began simply as a trolley park in the late 1800s. Trolley parks were areas created at "the end of the line" by trolley companies eager to entice riders to spend their spare time— and money—going

*Pathway to the Little Park of Memories*

*The Palisades' trolley park (shown here) opened to visitors in the 1800s.*

to the countryside with their families. For almost 10 years, the park successfully fulfilled this role while offering visitors wooded groves, picnic grounds, flower gardens, and breathtaking views of New York City. Late in 1907, though, the trolley company received an offer it couldn't refuse, and the park was sold to a man with a background in designing, managing, and remodeling theatrical and cultural institutions. This former bucolic setting soon transformed into a world-class amusement park.

On opening night as many as 3,000 people showed up to see the new park. Food, rides, entertainment acts, games of skill, and 15,000 electric lights were introduced into the reopened and renamed Palisades Amusement Park. A miniature train ride, a carousel, a man billed as the World's Most Daring High Diver, a Wild West show, and balloon flights across the Hudson River were just a few of the attractions. It was bigger, brasher, and brighter than the trolley park had ever been. Within a year, a zoo, puppet show, and Toboggan Slide roller coaster were added to the roster.

## Bathing in the Brine

The park was sold again a few years later to brothers Joseph and Nicholas Schenck, who renamed it after themselves in 1910 and brought in even more attractions. Their first season (seasons ran from May to September), the Schenck Brothers' Palisades Park's biggest draws were automobile races (since few people had their own cars at that time), the Sleigh Ride Coaster, and the Big Scenic Coaster. But the Schencks' masterpiece would come three years later.

Before June 1913, getting cool at the park just meant basking in the breezes off the Hudson River. But faced with growing competition from New York's Coney Island attractions (including a natural beach), the brothers came up with something big— they installed a "beach" of their own.

*Left and below: The "world's largest outdoor saltwater pool" at Palisades Park featured a swimming area and even a waterfall.*

Saltwater (a million gallons of it!) was pumped up from the Hudson River every day to fill the massive wave pool. (The same engineer who designed the carousel mechanism that makes horses go up and down designed the machinery to churn out waves.) As wide as a city block, the vast body of water was billed as the world's largest outdoor saltwater pool, allowed Palisades to advertise "surf bathing," and brought more people to the park.

## Say "Uncle!"

In 1935 the park, under new owners Irving and Jack Rosenthal, once again became Palisades Amusement Park. "Uncle" Irving (kids who called him that to his face were rewarded with a dollar bill) was an extremely imaginative promoter. The park thrived with his creative advertising gimmicks.

A new billboard (at the time, it was the world's largest moving sign) built on the cliffs included 32,000 lightbulbs. Matchbooks featured ads for the park—and provided free admission. To grab the interest of kids, coupons for the park appeared in comic books. Superman even became the park's official spokesperson. Discount tickets and special free admittance offers abounded: Uncle Irving knew that the trick was to get people inside the gates.

*Comic book ads like this one from 1961 grabbed kids' attention and brought them to the park.*

*Above: A 1930s postcard shows the Cyclone at Palisades Park. It became one of the most famous roller coasters in the world.*

*Above: After Palisades Park was demolished, these condos were built in its place.*

## All Things Must Come to an End

Once they were there, they'd spend even more money. According to legend, kids sneaked into the park for years through a hole in the fence; Rosenthal knew about the hole and ordered his men not to fix it.

Rosenthal's methods of measuring a day's success were also unorthodox: He relied on the trash at the end of the day. Park supervisor John Rinaldi remembered, "He'd walk the grounds, check the garbage, and say, 'We had a pretty good day.'"

New rides were always being rotated into the mix, too: The Lake Placid Bobsled coaster arrived in 1937. In 1944 the Skyrocket coaster (after having been damaged by fire) was rebuilt as the Cyclone, which became one of the most famous coasters in the world. Palisades Park was a mecca for roller coaster lovers.

The park's success eventually proved to be its downfall, however. While screams of excitement came from inside the park gates, cries of "foul!" came from outside them. Noise had always been an issue, and the traffic and parking situations had indisputably reached saturation levels. In 1967 rezoning propositions passed in the towns of Cliffside Park and neighboring Fort Lee. Irving Rosenthal, aging and in ailing health, didn't fight the new zoning. He bowed out gracefully and sold the property.

To the disappointment of untold numbers of kids and parents (including a group of schoolchildren who waged a write-in campaign to President Richard Nixon to keep the park open), the beloved summer stomping grounds closed its gates for the final time on September 12, 1971. Some attractions went to other amusement parks—some rides, such as the famous Cyclone roller coaster, were demolished. And condominium towers went up on the cleared acreage.

Twenty-seven years later, almost to the day, the Little Park of Memories was created, to the delight of an estimated 1,000 spectators at its dedication ceremony. One of this site's plaques states what may be the sentiment of many of those among the three generations of folks who savored summer seasons at the park: "Here we were happy, here we grew!"

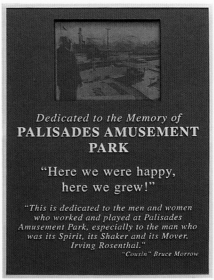

Dedicated to the Memory of
**PALISADES AMUSEMENT PARK**

"Here we were happy, here we grew!"

*"This is dedicated to the men and women who worked and played at Palisades Amusement Park, especially to the man who was its Spirit, its Shaker and its Mover, Irving Rosenthal."*
*"Cousin" Bruce Morrow*

*Today the Little Park of Memories and this plaque are all that's left of the great Palisades Park.*

# Beer Garden State

*Tired of lulls in your bar banter? These stories about beer brewers in New Jersey will give you something interesting to share.*

## Little Brew House on the Prairie

Hoboken is the site of America's first legal brewery. Around 1642, Dutch settler Aert Van Putten built the first house in Hoboken—which wouldn't be complete without a brew house, so he added a small one. But he and his fellow settlers quickly annoyed the local Lenni Lenape Indians. War broke out, and one night the Dutch massacred 80 native men, women, and children. The Lenni Lenape took revenge by burning down all of the colony's buildings…except the brewery. Was that on purpose? No one knows, but the brew house was still standing in 1663 when colonial governor Peter Stuyvesant issued it the first brewery charter in the nation.

*Prohibition supporters open barrels of New Jersey beer to pour into the Hudson River in 1929.*

## The Beer Barons

- During Prohibition in America (1920–33), many bootleggers ensured that New Jerseyans got their beer. In Trenton, "Beer Baron" Victor Cooper supplied the town's suds with the help of a close friend…police chief William Walter. When a clueless lieutenant busted Cooper's distillery in 1930, all 11 men arrested were immediately released without being fingerprinted, thanks to Chief Walter.

- Running Atlantic City was Enoch "Nucky" Johnson, who started off

*Above and right: A character based on the real Nucky Johnson was played by actor Steve Buscemi in the HBO show* Boardwalk Empire.

as a sheriff like his father, but then became a politician, brewery director, and racketeer. (Sound familiar? The character of Nucky Thompson in HBO's *Boardwalk Empire* is based on him.) Under Johnson's charge, Atlantic City's alcohol flowed freely and openly, unlike in other cities that kept their speakeasies underground. With his political influence, Johnson ensured that officials who tried to halt drinking or corruption got demoted and evidence was "lost."

- But the man behind the scenes, the one who supplied beer to the entire state,

*Max Hassel, the "Gentleman Beer Baron"*

was Max Hassel. Known as the "Gentleman Beer Baron," he didn't carry a gun and remained calm even when threatened. Once, when a local thug tried to commandeer his brewery in Camden, Hassel negotiated a partnership instead, banking on the fact that the other guy wouldn't be around long (he was soon shot). With his business acumen, Hassel gained control of all 16 of New Jersey's breweries during Prohibition. To avoid detection, he ran fire hoses underground along the sewer lines to siphon beer from his breweries to nearby warehouses where inspectors wouldn't find it. And by doling out bribes, Hassel didn't get hassled…until 1933, when he was shot in a case of mistaken identity.

## A Cold One in a Can

New Jersey won back its right to drink in 1933, but by then, the Gottfried Krueger Brewing Company in Newark (established in 1858) was struggling. It had closed all of its breweries but one, which barely survived Prohibition by manufacturing

near-beers and sodas. The company was losing out to bigger breweries such as Anheuser-Busch and Pabst, and its workers went on strike. But then the American Can Company approached Krueger with an offer: put beer in a can.

At the time, beer was sold only in bottles. Earlier attempts to can beer had been disastrous. Not only did the cans explode in trucks and stores from the pressure of the carbonation, but the beer reacted with canning metals and tasted awful. American Can engineers claimed to have fixed these problems. Although the big breweries were afraid to take the gamble, Krueger had nothing to lose: American Can offered to install canning machines free of charge at the brewery. If the canned beer succeeded, Krueger could buy the machines.

In January 1935, the brewery debuted Krueger's Finest Beer and its Cream Ale in cans—and customers and store owners loved it. American Can's engineers really had perfected the art of canning beer, and compared to glass, cans were lighter in weight, less fragile, and cheaper. By the end of the year, Krueger couldn't brew beer fast enough. Other companies quickly followed suit, and soon more than 30 breweries offered canned beer. (Krueger enjoyed success for almost three decades more, but finally folded in 1961, pushed out by the big breweries.)

*Krueger's cans—which first held cream ale and then beer—made canned drinks easier and cheaper to manufacture.*

## Craft Brew Comeback

If you've had Ballantine's India Pale Ale recently, you got a taste of the past… just like the founders intended. First brewed in 1878 by P. Ballantine & Sons Brewing Company in Newark, the beer is said to be America's first IPA (India Pale Ale). Beer lovers enjoyed it for a century before everything changed in the late 1960s, when American lagers like Coors became popular and craft beers like IPAs fell out of favor. The Ballantine company was sold and resold, and each time, its IPA's recipe changed significantly. "It was a shell of its former self," says master brewer Greg Deuhs of Pabst, which now owns the beer.

Eventually, craft beers made a comeback. Pabst wanted to revive Ballantine IPA in its original glory, just like it tasted back in the day. But without a 136-year-old recipe to follow, how could that be done? Science and some detective work. Deuhs reverse-engineered the beer through research and experimentation to determine the qualities—aroma, color, and bitterness—of the original beer. Two years and more than two dozen batches later, he found the perfect brew: Ballantine IPA re-debuted in 2014, and fans hope it's here to stay.

# Washington's Rubicon

*Cloak furling in the wind, standing majestically on one foot, George Washington led his troops across the Delaware River to win the Battle of Trenton, right? Well…something like that.*

## How the War Was Won

By Christmas Day 1776, the American Revolution was looking like a lost cause for the rebels. General George Washington, a hero to the Continental forces, had suffered a debilitating defeat a month earlier, when he lost New York City to the British, and his once-robust army had shrunk from 30,000 men to just 3,000. On Christmas night, Washington gathered his remaining men and crossed the Delaware River from Pennsylvania into New Jersey. The grueling crossing over the ice-choked river lasted ten hours, and only 2,400 soldiers made it, some without shoes on their feet. But in a miraculous turn of events, they marched to Trenton and surprised the enemy troops stationed there. The short, two-hour battle was a rout: 30 British loyalists were killed, 84 wounded, and nearly 900 captured—without a single loss to Washington's side. The victory gave the Continental forces the courage they needed to fight for another five years before the British conceded defeat. Dozens of eyewitness accounts of the crossing exist in soldiers' diaries and letters. But in the minds of most Americans, the crossing looks like a depiction in one painting: an 1851 canvas by Emanuel Leutze.

## Where's a Photographer When You Really Need One?

Today, Leutze's mammoth painting—12 feet by 21 feet—hangs in the Metropolitan Museum of Art in New York City. In the foreground stands Washington, one foot propped up in the lead boat. Behind him future president James Monroe clutches the Stars and Stripes. The boat's other occupants struggle to row toward the New Jersey shore. Leutze dressed the soldiers in garments from all over the colonies.

The striking image represents struggle in the face of insurmountable odds and the patriotism of the Americans. Unfortunately, it does not show what actually happened. For one, the crossing happened at night, not during the day, and it was sleeting, not partly cloudy. The boat is the wrong type, and the ice would have been submerged under the sluicing current. The flag Monroe holds is wrong, since the Stars and Stripes design was not adopted until 1777. And if Washington had stood on one leg in his boat like that, he would have gone headfirst into the river and America might still be part of the British Commonwealth.

*George Washington and his soldiers cross the Delaware River in the famous (though inaccurate) painting by Emanuel Leutze.*

## European History 101

Leutze didn't have historical accuracy in mind when he started his masterpiece, though. Born in Germany in 1816, he moved to the United States as a child. When the Revolution of 1848 broke out in Europe, he returned to Germany to support the democratic cause. And how does an artist aid a revolution? With art, of course. Leutze took inspiration from the struggles of his adopted country and used the image of Washington to capture the spirit of freedom.

He began work on the painting in 1848, but as he painted, the European revolutions failed, and it was with a sense of desperation that he finished in 1850. *Washington Crossing the Delaware* stood as a symbol of the eleventh-hour miracle that had saved America's revolution and, Leutze believed, might still save Germany's. The original painting found its way to the Bremen Art Museum in Germany, but was destroyed in 1942 during a bombing raid by the British Royal Air Force.

Fortunately, Leutze had painted a full-size copy in 1851 that he sent to the United States, where it was an instant hit. The painting was first displayed in the Rotunda of the National Capitol and was eventually donated to the Metropolitan Museum's permanent collection. In 1998 New Jersey chose the image for the back of its state quarter, creating the first currency with George Washington on both sides. And today, despite its inaccuracies, it's still the

*Emanuel Leutze's painting inspired hundreds of replicas: everything from postcards and sculpture (far left and below) to the engraving on New Jersey's state quarter.*

primary image most Americans have of that important day back in 1776.

## Life Imitates Art

The painting also inspired a group of men to create a whole new tradition. On a blustery Christmas Day in 1953, seven men in an open boat crossed the Delaware in full Revolutionary dress. Led by Saint John Terrell, who would continue to play George Washington every Christmas for decades, these men started the modern tradition of reenacting the rebels' historic crossing. Of course, not every year goes off without a hitch. In 2000 police grounded the trip for safety reasons; it was just too cold.

So the history buffs instead pushed their boat along Pennsylvania's shore instead. In past years, the reenactors have marched over the nearby bridge instead of rowing, and once forded the Delaware on foot after a drought left the water level so low the boats couldn't float.

They still do it today. If you trudge out to Washington Crossing State Park in Hopewell Township next Christmas, you'll see reenactors struggling to maintain the poses of Leutze's painting as they push across the river, anachronistic flag and all.

*Right and above: History buffs reenact Washington's landing in New Jersey on December 25, 2009.*

# The Real Rocky

*Sylvester Stallone's Rocky movies were based on a real-life person...*
*but he wasn't from Philadelphia—he was from New Jersey.*

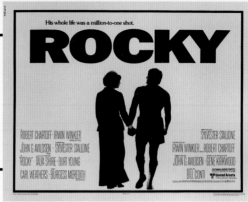

## Putting on the Golden Gloves

Everyone's heard of Rocky Balboa, but only true boxing fans know about Chuck Wepner, the real-life boxer on whom the Rocky movies were based. Born in Bayonne in 1939, Wepner cut his teeth as a Jersey nightclub bouncer. He was tough—just ask the upstarts unfortunate enough to receive his services—and soon gained a reputation for his fearlessness, determination, and high tolerance for pain.

As a young man Wepner joined the Marine Corps, where he first learned to box to earn extra time off. When he finished his stint in the military, Wepner fought in the amateur boxing circuit on the weekends and evenings. He could never quit his day job to box full-time and could train only at night, but at a friend's suggestion, one year he threw his hat into the ring for a Golden Gloves match—and won. He went on to fight professionally, but making ends meet was hard. While other boxers could spend their days training, Wepner still had to earn a living at regular jobs: he worked as a bouncer, liquor salesman, and security guard throughout his professional boxing career. He fought tough, up-and-coming contenders but always remained in the background.

## The Bayonne Bleeder

Eventually, though, Wepner became famous for his ability to take a beating. In fact, he became so famous that he earned the nickname "the Bayonne Bleeder." He wasn't about finesse; he was about being the last one standing. And after a respectable number of wins, he finally got a huge opportunity in 1975: Chuck Wepner would take on Muhammad Ali for the world heavyweight title. This was his big chance, and he leaped at it. But the rest of the world laughed—no way was this nobody going to last against the Champ! Some experts predicted that the fight would last only three rounds, if that long at all.

Well, the crowd was right in one respect: Wepner did lose to Ali. But he shocked everyone by going 15 rounds—even sending the Champ crashing to the canvas with a wicked right hook in the ninth round. The referee stopped the fight out of concern for Wepner's health with only 19 seconds to go. Despite taking a dangerous beating from Ali, Wepner simply wouldn't give up on his own.

He retired in 1978, after having fought not only the great Muhammad Ali, but also Sonny Liston, George Foreman, and Andre the

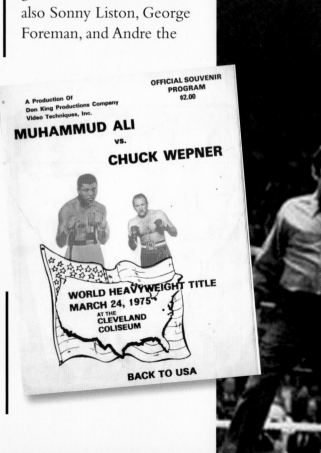

*Wepner throws a right punch at opponent James Sullivan during the 1964 Golden Gloves match.*

Giant. Wepner wrote an autobiography entitled *Toe to Toe with Any Foe* and was eventually inducted into the New Jersey Boxing Hall of Fame (with a professional record of 35–14–2; 17 of his wins were by knockout).

## Yo, Chuckie?

Boxing fans around the country caught that 1975 fight between Wepner and Ali, if only to see Wepner get creamed. And New York actor Michael Sylvester Enzio Stallone was no exception. A dropout of the University of Miami's drama program, Stallone made his living acting in off-Broadway plays and the occasional small film; but he also

liked boxing. Stallone wound up at the Wepner–Ali fight and was inspired by the underdog's performance in the 15-round brawl to write a screenplay that became the hit film *Rocky*, the story of a down-on-his-luck tough guy who makes it big in boxing. Stallone sold the screenplay for $150,000 and played the lead role in the movie, which was a smash. *Rocky* won the Oscar for Best Picture in 1976, and Stallone himself was nominated for his performance. Many say this film was the best work of his career. The film spawned a franchise and launched five sequels.

*Sylvester Stallone was nominated for an Oscar in 1976 for his performance in* Rocky.

## Still Fighting—in Court

But Wepner never saw a cent of the reported millions of dollars the Rocky movies generated, so in 2003 he sued Stallone. When Stallone sold the script back in the 1970s, he called Wepner to tell him about it. Over the years, Wepner claims that Stallone promised compensation in a variety of forms, including a bit part in *Rocky II* that wound up on the cutting-room floor. Wepner claimed that after years of promises and the use of his name to promote the Rocky series, he had been cheated. He told the *Philadelphia Inquirer* that "after 28 years, even an ex-fighter starts to figure maybe this guy is not going to keep his word."

The real-life tough guy wanted compensation for all the times Stallone used his name during the promotion of the films. Wepner's lawyer told CBS News that "Stallone has been using Chuck's name—and continues to this day—in promoting the Rocky franchise without any permission or compensation." In September 2004 Stallone's lawyers tried to have the case thrown out of court, but they were unsuccessful. In 2006 the two finally settled the lawsuit for an undisclosed amount.

*Wepner lasted an impressive 15 rounds against Muhammad Ali in 1975, taking hit after hit (left) but ultimately losing the heavyweight title.*

# On the Banks of the Old Raritan

*Rutgers' school song tells you where it is, but it doesn't tell you much about the university itself. Here's a crash course on the great academic institution.*

## The Where, When, and How

- When it was first founded, Rutgers was located in New Brunswick, along the Raritan River in Middlesex County. Originally chartered on November 10, 1766, as Queen's College, Rutgers is the eighth-oldest institution of higher education in the United States. Since then, the university has expanded to 29 divisions, 12 undergraduate colleges, 11 graduate schools, and 3 schools offering both undergraduate and graduate degrees. In all, Rutgers offers more than 200 bachelor's, master's, and doctoral and professional degree programs.

- Queen's College was named for Charlotte Sophia of Mecklenburg-Strelitz, queen consort (that is, wife) of King George III. The name was changed to Rutgers College in 1825 to honor Colonel Henry Rutgers, a hero of the Revolutionary War and supporter of "benevolent causes." He donated a bell and $5,000, which was enough to keep the school from closing its doors. The school became a university in 1924, and an act of the state legislature in 1954 put on the final touches, designating it as Rutgers, the State University of New Jersey.

## One University, Many Colleges

- Today Rutgers University has more than 65,000 students on three campuses. The main grounds are in New Brunswick and Piscataway, which is home to Rutgers, Douglass, Cook, and Livingston Colleges. There are additional Rutgers campuses in Camden and Newark.

*Above: The the main campus at Rutgers in 1913*

*Left: The Olde Queens gate welcomes visitors to Rutgers University.*

- Rutgers College is the flagship institution, with an enrollment of more than 11,000 undergraduate students. Douglass College, with approximately 3,000 students, dates back to 1918 and is the largest women's college in the United States. Cook College is a land-grant college with 3,200 students and a focus on agriculture and environmental sciences. It became a separate branch in 1973, having evolved from the Rutgers Scientific School. Livingston College was founded in 1969 as the first coed liberal arts college at Rutgers. It currently has 3,900 students and is committed to diversity, equality of opportunity, and educational innovation.

*Among Rutgers' greatest contributions: Cheez-Whiz.*

**Best thing that can happen to burgers and hot dogs:**

*Cheez Whiz 'em!*

- In 1793 a resolution to merge Queen's College with the College of New Jersey (now Princeton University) lost by one vote.
- A Rutgers professor "discovered" Cheez-Whiz at the school's Center for Advanced Food Technology.
- Rutgers professor Selman A. Waksman was awarded the 1952 Nobel Prize in Physiology or Medicine for his discovery of Streptomycin, the first antibiotic to treat tuberculosis successfully.

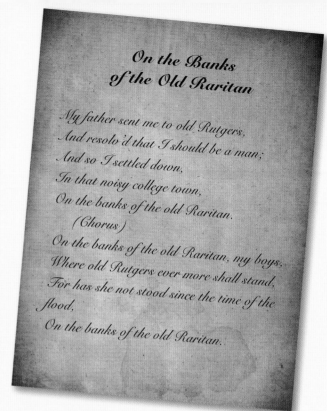

*On the Banks of the Old Raritan*

*My father sent me to old Rutgers,*
*And resolv'd that I should be a man;*
*And so I settled down,*
*In that noisy college town,*
*On the banks of the old Raritan.*
*(Chorus)*
*On the banks of the old Raritan, my boys,*
*Where old Rutgers ever more shall stand,*
*For has she not stood since the time of the flood,*
*On the banks of the old Raritan.*

## Alma Mater

The Rutgers alma mater, "On the Banks of the Old Raritan," dates from 1872. It opens as follows:

*My father sent me to old Rutgers,*
*And resolv'd that I should be a man;*
*And so I settled down,*
*In that noisy college town,*
*On the banks of the old Raritan.*
*(Chorus)*
*On the banks of the old Raritan, my boys,*
*Where old Rutgers ever more shall stand,*
*For has she not stood since the time of the flood,*
*On the banks of the old Raritan.*

Rutgers College went coed in 1972 and is now about 52 percent female. In 1990, the "my boys" in the first line of the song's chorus was changed to "my friends," but the opening wish "that I should be a man" remains.

## R.U. Trivia

- In the 1770s, classes were held at a tavern called the Sign of the Red Lion.
- William Franklin, New Jersey's last colonial governor and the illegitimate son of Benjamin Franklin (his mother is unknown), signed the Rutgers charter.
- Henry Rutgers's most famous quotation was "Don't let your studies interfere with your education."
- The Rutgers motto is *Sol iustitiae et occidentem illustra* (Sun of righteousness, shine upon the West also).

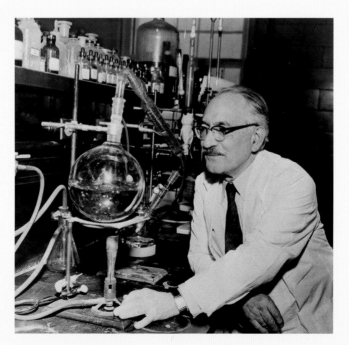

*Selman Abrham Waksman works in his laboratory in 1953.*

# This Island Is My Land!

*From Cal-i-for-nia to Ellis Island… (New Jersey, that is.)*

## Drawing a Line in the Sand

You may think that Ellis Island is in New York, but you'd be wrong. The main immigration building on Ellis Island, now a museum, does have a New York address. But since 1998, the kitchen and laundry facilities of the main building and the rest of the island, including the docks where tourists arrive, are actually located in New Jersey. How did this place come to have such an identity crisis? It's just the last stage of a centuries-long border dispute between the two states.

The Hudson River forms the border between New York and New Jersey as it flows through New York Harbor and out to the Atlantic Ocean. But just where in the river does one state turn into another? The first border battle started in 1801, when Alexander Hamilton built a pier in Jersey City that pointed out into the Hudson River toward New York. New York City informed Hamilton that his pier, and anything else extending into the Hudson River, was part of the state of New York. New Jersey disagreed, and the dispute kicked off 30 years of squabbles and court battles. Finally, in 1834, the two states signed a compact agreeing that the border between the states runs down the middle of the Hudson, with the exception of a few now-famous islands in the river—namely, Liberty and Ellis Islands.

*Left: A nineteenth-century map of New York*

The 1834 agreement gave New York jurisdiction over Ellis and Liberty Islands even though they clearly fall on New Jersey's side of the river. At the time, it didn't matter much. Ellis Island was three acres of rock with an army installment on it. Bedloe's Island (renamed Liberty Island in 1956) was a completely uninteresting lump until 1886, when the Statue of Liberty was placed there.

*The Statue of Liberty faces New York, with Jersey City and Ellis Island in the background. More than 12 million immigrants passed through Ellis Island between 1892 and 1954.*

*Above: The second Ellis Island Immigration Station opened in 1900.*

## Ellis Island Expansion

The federal government set up its main immigrant-processing center on Ellis Island in 1892. Between then and 1954, when it closed, some 12 million immigrants came through this facility—40 percent of all Americans can trace their heritage back to this rock in New York Harbor.

To accommodate that number of immigrants, the U.S. Army Corps of Engineers built up the island, which gradually expanded between 1892 and 1954 to its present size of 27.5 acres. The additional land made room for a ferry slip, a hospital, and various administrative buildings. But since this land was not part of Ellis Island in 1834, it wasn't clear which state could officially lay claim to it.

## Tag, You're It!

Where the official state line was didn't seem to matter all that much until 1992, when Terry Collins, a national park ranger, lost part of his leg while working on the landfill area of Ellis Island. He sued Promark Products, the makers of the equipment he was using, who in turn sued the federal government for not properly training Collins. Here's where it gets tricky: the State of New York allows such a countersuit, but the State of New Jersey does not.

In order to avoid liability, the federal government said that the part of Ellis Island Collins was working on was actually in New Jersey, not New York. The 1834 pact said Ellis Island belonged to New York, but it also said that all the underwater land surrounding it was New Jersey's. Therefore the expanded island, since it was not part of the original exemption, must be in New Jersey. The Federal District Court of Manhattan didn't buy it. The judge ruled that all the dry land on Ellis Island was New York's, and all the underwater land was New Jersey's. With this logic, you could sit on a pier in New York and have bits of New Jersey wash up over your ankles.

*Immigrants wait in line to be processed at Ellis Island in 1910.*

## Hey, Wait a Minute!

Perhaps incensed by the Collins ruling, New Jersey filed suit against New York in 1993 for custody of the 24 added acres of Ellis Island—a case that made it all the way to the U.S. Supreme Court in 1996. New Jersey's case rested almost entirely on the pact of 1834, while New York claimed that Ellis Island was, and always had been, a cultural part of New York. To support its claim, New York's lawyers argued that the immigrants going through Ellis Island were going to New York, not New Jersey. The way you could tell, they said, was that the immigrants on the boats coming to Ellis Island were facing New York, so the island was therefore part of New York. Since no poll had been taken of the immigrants at the time, the court dismissed both of these claims.

Instead of rendering a decision, the Supreme Court assigned an arbitrator named Paul Verkuil (a New Yorker) to evaluate the case and make a recommendation. His decision came on April 1, 1997. In light of the evidence, Verkuil decided that New York had no legal claim to the landfill areas of Ellis Island. In the interest of fairness, he recommended that New York be awarded approximately five acres, since the original island is now landlocked. The compromise pleased nobody. Both states wanted all of the additional land. (One annoyed citizen even wrote the *New York Times* suggesting that since New York and New Jersey were being so immature, the court should give the island to Connecticut instead.)

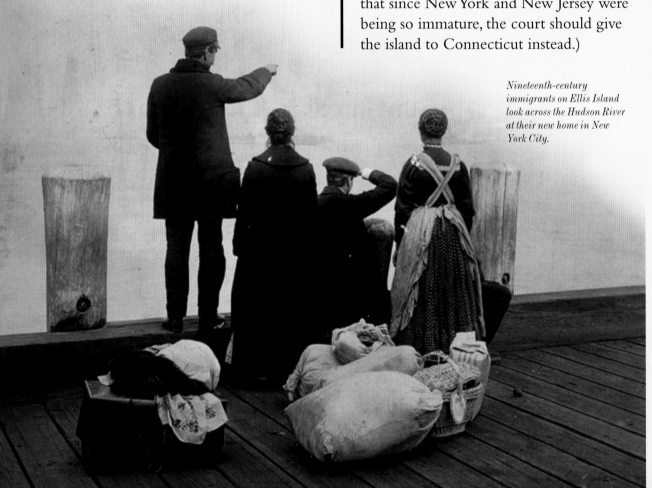

*Nineteenth-century immigrants on Ellis Island look across the Hudson River at their new home in New York City.*

*Supreme Court Justice Antonin Scalia.*

## Welcome to the State of New Jersey

So back to the Supreme Court the case went. On May 26, 1998, the court voted 6–3 to divide the island and award New Jersey all of the landfill acres. (State loyalty played no part in this case. Antonin Scalia, the only New Jerseyan on the court, voted to keep the island in New York.) Based on this decision, the official state line now runs smack through the middle of the main immigration building.

Triumphant, New Jersey's governor, Christine Todd Whitman, sported a T-shirt saying, "Ellis Island, NJ" in bold letters. The U.S. Postal Service added a New Jersey zip code for the island. New Jersey raised its flag on Ellis Island on the Fourth of July that year, thumbing its nose at New York.

So what's the upshot of all this legal wrangling? What does it mean for the island now that it's (mostly) in New Jersey? Absolutely nothing. Ellis Island is owned by the federal government and has been since 1800. It's a national park. Other than a few thousand dollars a year in sales taxes, all New Jersey really got from the ordeal was bragging rights.

# Jersey Boys and Girls

*New Jerseyans just love to talk about their state.*

"You're in the shadow of New York, always trying to prove yourself…It's like you're the redheaded stepchild."

**—Kevin Smith**

"There's a directness and a feistiness to being from Jersey."

**—Ali Larter, actress**

*Kevin Smith*

"Out here [in Los Angeles] it's strange because everyone always says, 'You're totally from, like, Jersey.' I'm like, 'What is that supposed to mean?'"

**—Laura Prepon, actress**

"Your best bet when driving in Jersey: Move it or lose it. It's the pokey Pennsylvanians that tend to gum everything up, so step lively, and we're not kidding around with our left lane—if you can't hack it, move over."

**—Sarah D. Bunting, writer and co-founder of Television Without Pity**

"New Jersey shaped who and what I am. Growing up in Jersey gave you all the advantages of New York, but you were in its shadow. Anyone who's come from here will tell you that same story."

**—Jon Bon Jovi**

"I love Jersey…I had a great time down there in Princeton doing *Anger Management*. Being a Jersey boy, you know [it]…was really something. I'm one of the few living people who can say they saw Dick Kazmaier play football live."

**—Jack Nicholson**

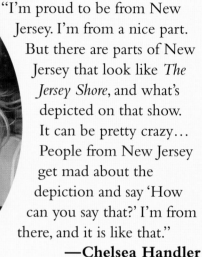

"I'm proud to be from New Jersey. I'm from a nice part. But there are parts of New Jersey that look like *The Jersey Shore*, and what's depicted on that show. It can be pretty crazy… People from New Jersey get mad about the depiction and say 'How can you say that?' I'm from there, and it is like that."

**—Chelsea Handler**

*Chelsea Handler*

*Jon Bon Jovi*

*Jack Nicholson*

# Things that Go Bump in the Night

*Don't be afraid—it's only Uncle John's collection of spooky specters, awful apparitions, and haunted high jinks in the Garden State.*

## Jenny, a Young Colonial Girl

**Haunted Hangout:** Hope, Warren County

**Spooky Sight:** A young girl floating around the lakes and cliff, crying out for her father.

**The Spectral Scoop:** There are several versions of the story, but the most popular comes from a 1747 account of a Swedish missionary, Sven Roseen. Nine-year-old Jenny lived in a house beneath a high cliff that overlooked a lake. One day Jenny accompanied her father to the high cliff to pick berries while her father collected wood. When Jenny noticed some unfriendly Lenape tribe members approaching, she cried out in warning to her father. Possibly afraid that his daughter's virtue (and her life) might be in danger, Jenny's father yelled, "Jump, Jenny, jump!" An obedient child, Jenny leapt off the rocky cliff and fell to her death. But even though her body was crushed by the fall, her spirit stayed on. To this day, her plaintive voice can supposedly be heard and her ghostly figure seen around the cliffs in the Jenny Jump State Forest that was named for her.

## William Chaplain

**Haunted Hangout:** New Monmouth, Monmouth County

**Spooky Sight:** A young soldier, dressed in colonial attire, playing mournful ballads on his flute.

**The Spectral Scoop:** Local legend has it that William Chaplain, a 17-year-old flute enthusiast, spied on the Americans for the British during the Revolutionary War. The patriots discovered his treachery and shot him in the back within the sight of the British. Many thought those bullets had been the end of young William, but in the late evenings in New Monmouth,

*Above and right: Jenny Jump State Forest*

54

residents claim that this ghostly traitor sings sad ballads and plays tunes on a flute.

## Robert Erskine

**Haunted Hangout:** Ringwood State Park, Passaic County

**Spooky Sight:** A ghostly figure who sits on his grave, waves a lantern, follows people around, thumps around in his mansion, and holds a ball of blue light.

**Spectral Scoop:** It's not just the chills and clammy sensations or the doors that lock themselves that persuade many visitors that Erskine haunts the Ringwood property. In life, Erskine had managed the American Iron Company's facilities in Ringwood. He was appointed by George Washington to be the surveyor general for the Continental Army during the War for Independence. Sadly, in 1780, he died young after catching a cold while working on New Jersey maps.

Over the years, many people claimed to have seen the ghost of General Erskine, but what caused his spirit to linger remains a mystery. Some say the appearance of ghostly Erskine is related to the possibility that his manor and iron ore mines may have defaced nearby sacred Native American lands and cursed his spirit.

*Above: Ringwood State Park, said to be haunted by a Revolutionary War–era mapmaker named Robert Erskine.*

*Right: One of Erskine's eighteenth-century maps shows New York's Orange and Rockland Counties.*

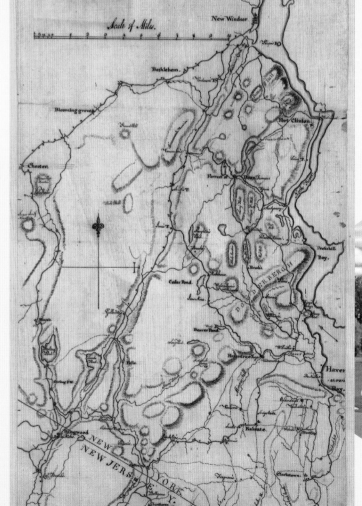

## A Decapitated Hessian Soldier

**Haunted Hangout:** Kenilworth, Union County

**Spooky Sight:** A galloping headless rider on horseback.

**Spectral Scoop:** Washington Irving may have made Tarrytown famous with his ghost story "The Legend of Sleepy Hollow," but some say that his inspiration for the menacing Headless Horseman came from a New Jersey legend. During the War for Independence, a Hessian soldier (Germans hired to fight for the British) had his head taken off by the Continental Army. Some say it was sliced off—others say a cannonball did the foul deed. Ever since, his headless form and his horse continue to gallop across what is now the Galloping Hills Golf Course. The story of the Headless Hessian was popular during Irving's time, so some historians speculate that he took a little literary license and relocated the tale.

*The Galloping Hills Golf Course*

## An Unnamed, One-Armed Railway Worker

**Haunted Hangout:** Chester, Morris County

**Spooky Sight:** Green light bobbing up and down over the railroad tracks.

**Spectral Scoop:** One of New Jersey's most famous ghost stories is of the Hookerman: a nameless railroad worker who lost his life while repairing the tracks at night. When his arm became stuck and could not be freed, an unexpected train mowed him down. A morbid tale indeed, but what makes his story even eerier is that the man's body was found, but his arm and lantern had completely disappeared.

Since the accident, people have reported a bobbing green light that hovers over the Central Railroad of New Jersey's former tracks. Some say the Hookerman's body is looking for his lost arm; others say it's his ghostly arm that still clutches a lantern while looking for his body. But no matter what body part you prefer, the tale of the Hookerman is so popular that he even has a beer named after him: the Long Valley Pub and Brewery created Hookerman's Light, an American wheat ale, in his honor.

## ESTHER ALLEN, "THE PARTYING GHOST"

**Haunted Hangout:** The Southern Mansion, Cape May County

**Spooky Sight:** Phantom female who dances, laughs, rustles her petticoat, and leaves behind traces of her perfume.

*Above: The Long Valley Pub and Brewery in Chester offers a wheat ale named after the Hookerman.*

**Spectral Scoop:** While many ghosts possess tragic pasts, here is the story of a ghost who stayed behind because she missed having a good time. As the niece of wealthy industrialist George Allen, Esther was able to enjoy all the privileges of affluence. Her uncle spared no expense in constructing a palatial seaside mansion in 1863, primarily for entertaining guests with extravagant parties. When Esther died she wasn't ready to stop her good time so, the legend says, she hung around her old home, now a bed-and-breakfast called the Southern Mansion. Esther currently entertains the owner and guests alike with numerous sightings of her lively spirit. Occasionally laughter can be heard from several empty rooms, and if observers are lucky, they'll catch a glimpse of her dancing from room to room.

*Right: The Southern Mansion is said to be the haunted hangout of Esther Allen's ghost.*

# They Did What?

*These New Jerseyans claim they have a good explanation for their irresponsible behavior, but we're not so sure. You be the judge.*

## Brawl in the Family

**Who:** Thomas Connors, mayor of Seaside Park

**Where:** Seaside Heights, a neighboring town

**What Happened:** In 2010 Mayor Connors and his adult children visited a restaurant and club called Hemingway's Café. First, Connors's 23-year-old son Anthony got kicked out. As bouncers "escorted" Anthony outside, he tried to fight them and force his way back into the building. Police on the street saw the melee and arrested him. His sister Lindsay, age 22, had followed Anthony outside, and she began hitting one of the officers on the arm and chest to get him to release her brother. She was also taken into custody. Finally, their dad was pulled outside by bar staff. When he saw his kids getting cuffed, he turned into an overprotective papa, tried to interfere, and was also arrested.

**Excuse:** Mayor Connors, who did have a cut above his eye, claimed he'd been defending his daughter from obnoxious guys inside. When they assaulted him, his son jumped in to help. He says he was fighting…but for a good cause.

**Outcome:** Connors remained mayor through 2011, but the incident sparked headlines saying that, on the Jersey Shore, even the mayor's a brawler.

## Streaker of the Year

**Who:** Fifth-grade teacher Mark Bringhurst

**Where:** Berlin

**What Happened:** During the 2011–12 school year, Bringhurst was honored with the title of Teacher of the Year at the elementary school in Vineland where he'd taught for eight years. Unfortunately, he dishonored himself soon after. In 2012 police were called around 8 p.m. to an apartment complex where a witness saw a man run through the parking lot naked, hop in a car, and speed off. The same man had apparently done the same thing there before. An officer, on a hunch, checked an adult bookstore nearby, and sure enough, there was a car outside and a man inside that matched the witness's descriptions.

**Excuse:** At first, Bringhurst denied being at the complex. Then the 40-year-old said he'd streaked through the complex but hadn't meant for anyone to see. The officer reported, "He did it on a dare. He explained he met someone online who likes to dare him to run through some sort of parking lot naked." Bringhurst admitted he'd streaked once before, at the same complex. According to the officer who asked why he chose that particular place, "the first time he did it, he just happened to be near there when he was dared. He said on this occasion he did it out of familiarity."

**Outcome:** Bringhurst was convicted on charges of lewd behavior and was fired.

*The Seaside Heights pier*

## Tanorexic

**Who:** Patricia Krentcil, mother of five

**Where:** Nutley

**What Happened:** It's obvious from one glance at Krentcil's dark leathery skin that she tans at salons "excessively." That's her choice. But in 2012, her five-year-old daughter Anna went to school with a burn on her leg and said it was from "tanning with Mommy." Because it's illegal for children under age 14 to use tanning salons in New Jersey, Krentcil was arrested and charged with child endangerment. While she awaited trial, the media dubbed her the "Tanorexic Mom," and tanning salons posted her picture to warn staff not to admit her. Krentcil became national news...and the butt of jokes about Jersey residents who over-tan.

**Excuse:** Krentcil denies that she would ever bring her child into a tanning bed, and no one saw Anna in the stand-up booth with her. There was evidence of burns on the girl's skin, though. Her mom claims that Anna got burned the way most kids do—by playing outside in the sun.

**Outcome:** A grand jury declined to indict Krentcil, though some people still think it was irresponsible of her to let Anna be sunburned so badly.

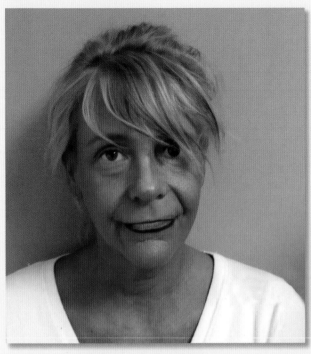

*Above and below: The Tanorexic mom used tanning beds like this one to over-tan.*

## Let It Pass

**Who:** 72-year-old Daniel Collins

**Where:** Teaneck

**What Happened:** In 2012 Collins was arrested in his apartment for allegedly threatening to shoot his neighbor. The troubles between Collins and the 47-year-old man had started long before that, when the two began an ongoing dispute about noise. It came to a head when an enraged Collins grabbed a gun, ran outside his apartment, pointed it at the resident, and said, "I'm going to put a hole in your head."

**Excuse:** What set Collins off? Supposedly, the neighbor passed gas loudly in front of his door. Collins said he "confronted" the flatulent man (who didn't want to be identified) but denied having threatened him with a gun.

**Outcome:** Police arrived, and upon searching Collins's car, they discovered a .32 revolver just like the one the neighbor described. Collins was arrested but, at last check, had been released to await trial for multiple charges, including "making terroristic threats."

**Moral:** You'd better watch where you let one loose.

# Books, Bounty Hunters, and the Burg

*Janet Evanovich has created a series of best-selling novels set in Trenton that feature a bounty-hunter babe named Stephanie Plum. So what's the story behind those stories?*

## You Can't Take the Jersey Out of the Girl

Star of her own literary mystery series, the fictional Stephanie Plum is a hilarious bounty hunter from Trenton. An unemployed discount-lingerie buyer, Stephanie was forced by hard economic times (and the end of her disastrous marriage) to work as a bounty hunter for her sleazy cousin Vinnie, a bail bond agent. Despite keeping her gun in the cookie jar and not a holster, Stephanie jumps right in and tracks down some of Trenton's shadiest characters. Her adventures in crime fighting are matched only by her colorful family, the sexy men in (and out of) her life, and her faithful companion Rex, her pet hamster.

The author of the Stephanie Plum series of books is also a Jersey girl: South River's Janet Evanovich. She started out writing romance, but in 1994

launched her first Stephanie saga, *One for the Money*. The book's mixture of serious crime, humor, and romance won a slew of devoted fans, who quickly gobbled up each new volume, turning Evanovich's books into a worldwide phenomenon. *Top Secret Twenty-One*, published in June 2014, shot to number one on the *New York Times* best-seller list.

*Left: Stephanie Plum (Katherine Heigl) and Joe Morelli (Jason O'Mora) keep an eye out for criminals in 2012's* One for the Money.

*Below: Katherine Heigl takes aim as Stephanie Plum.*

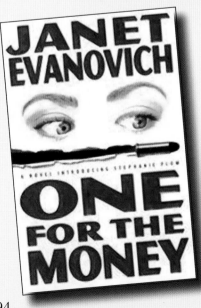

*Rex, a hamster like this one, is among Stephanie Plum's companions.*

*The Chambersburg section of Trenton became the stomping grounds of Stephanie Plum.*

## You Can Go Burg Again

Evanovich has stated that setting the books in Trenton contributes both to the comedy and the gritty crime elements in her novels. Jersey food, Jersey traffic, Jersey folks, and Jersey energy in general are, she feels, a key to Stephanie Plum's success. Life in Plum's neighborhood can be difficult, but according to Evanovich the important thing is that it's never bland.

Evanovich set her story in the Chambersburg section of town (called the Burg for short), but her first connection to Trenton's old Italian–German neighborhood wasn't a happy one. After her family moved to Mercerville, Evanovich's father became very ill.

He spent a lot of time recovering at St. Francis Medical Center, located on the edge of the Burg, and Evanovich took the train to visit him. As she sat with her dad, she could look out from the high hospital windows down into the neighborhood. She liked what she saw.

*Marsilio's in Trenton helped Janet Evanovich get into the New Jersey mindset to write her books.*

The area between Hamilton and Chambers Streets contained well-kept houses with lots of delis, bakeries, and Italian restaurants. It didn't exactly look like her hometown of South River, but it reminded her of it just the same. As Evanovich spent more time strolling through the area and meeting the people, she felt comforted and comfortable. This was a place where the residents knew each other and watched out for each other. Memories of the Burg stayed with her long after she graduated from Douglass College, married Pete Evanovich, and raised her daughter Alex and son Peter.

When Evanovich began to write about a bounty hunter who worried about hair, her makeup, and fugitives on the run, she looked for the setting of a tight-knit community with strong values and traditions. Evanovich was living in a Virginia suburb at the time but didn't feel it had enough character. Instead she figured that "you can't go wrong with New Jersey," and turned back to Chambersburg.

Writing a mystery series required research, so Evanovich returned to Trenton and did her homework. When she wasn't eating vodka rigatoni at Marsilio's Restaurant, she was visiting the Clinton Avenue police station to learn the ropes. Three-quarters of the way through her first mystery book, Evanovich was stumped by her fictional crime—until one of her Trenton friends, a police officer, stepped in to solve it so she could finish the book.

## Meanwhile, Back in New Hampshire...

Evanovich's connection with Trenton runs so deep that fans are often surprised to learn that she writes the series from her home in bucolic Hanover, New Hampshire. There, her novels are the foundation of a family company, Evanovich Inc. Janet writes the novels; daughter Alex is the Webmaster for her Web site; Janet's husband Peter is general manager; and her son Peter Jr. handles the company's finances.

Will Evanovich ever move to Trenton? Not in the near future. The creator of Stephanie Plum has explained that though her heart belongs to Jersey, if she lived there, she'd never get any writing done. She'd always be at the mall.

*Janet Evanovich in 2010*

# Don't Be Afraid

*New Jersey is home to some creepy crawly creatures that seem to inspire a lot of fear. Don't worry, though. They won't hurt you…probably.*

### Bats

There are nine species of bats found in New Jersey, but you don't have to worry about any of them trying to bite your neck. They all eat insects. To test your bravery, the best place to see bats is the Hibernia mine in Rockaway. It houses up to 30,000 of them.

### Dragonflies

Lots of dragonflies (over 175 species!) make their home in the Garden State. Even though their names are scary (e.g., devil's darning needle), they're perfectly harmless to humans. They're deadly to other insects, though—especially mosquitoes, one of their favorite snacks.

### Horseshoe Crabs

Every year in late spring, horseshoe crabs flock to the Jersey Shore for mating season. Beachgoers are often frightened by the crabs' appearance: seven spidery legs, a hard domed shell, and a long spiky tail. (By the way, horseshoe crabs are not technically crabs. Crabs are crustaceans, and horseshoe crabs are merostomatans.) But rest assured, horseshoe crabs have no claws to pinch and no teeth to bite. The worst they can do is startle you.

# Inside, Outside, Upside Down

*You want thrills? You want twists and turns? You want speed? Well, New Jersey's got some of the fastest, tallest, and scariest roller coasters in the country!*

### Great White

**Where?** Morey's Piers, Wildwood
Located near the Spencer Avenue Pier, the Great White first plunges riders 25 feet into a dark tunnel under the boardwalk. Then, before they know it, they are plummeting down a second, larger hill (125 feet!) and reaching speeds of more than 50 mph. According to Morey's, the Great White is one of the biggest wooden roller coasters in North America—it has over 3,300 feet of track. It may not be as flashy as some of its steelier cousins, but the Great White is Morey's most popular ride.

### Hell Cat

**Where?** Clementon Amusement Park, Clementon
Built in 2004, the Hell Cat replaced Clementon's other famous wooden roller coaster, the Jack Rabbit. Even though patrons were sad to see the old model go, they were thrilled by the brand-new coaster's first drop—105 feet with the steepest vertical angle (62 degrees) on a wooden coaster in North America. The ride reaches a top speed of 56 mph and features two more big drops—82 feet and 65 feet—before it's through.

### Superman Ultimate Flight

**Where?** Six Flags Great Adventure, Jackson
It's a bird! It's a plane! It's a…person on a roller coaster? Riders don't sit on this roller coaster—they fly headfirst, just like Superman. Passengers are strapped in and lie horizontally in hanging cars. This 115-foot-tall, pretzel-shaped thrill ride reaches speeds of 60 mph as it zips through spirals, highly banked curves, and a 360-degree in-line roll. Be warned: the red cape is not included.

*The Great White's builders ran out of room on the pier, so they constructed the coaster right on Wildwood's beach.*

## Great Nor'Easter

**Where?** Morey's Piers, Wildwood
Located on the 25th Avenue Pier, the Great Nor'Easter, named for the vicious storms that tear up the Atlantic seaboard, lives up to its moniker. It's an inverted coaster, meaning that the cars hang from the track and the riders dangle beneath them.

Made of more than 2,100 feet of steel, this ride is 150 feet tall and speeds along at over 50 mph. Riders go upside down four times. Best of all, the ride hovers high over the Raging Waters waterpark, bringing passengers so close to the ground that they feel like they're going to crash into the pools below.

*Riders take the plunge on the Great Nor'Easter.*

## Jersey Speak

**A.C.**
This abbreviation stands for Atlantic City (which may be pronounced 'Lanic City), not air conditioning.

**Benny**
A term of obscure origin, benny refers to a day-tripping tourist at the Jersey Shore; usually seen on bumper stickers that say "Benny go home."

**Joisey**
How out-of-staters pronounce Jersey. People from the Garden State never say it that way.

**Jug Handle**
A genius civil engineering advance that allows motorists to make left turns from the right lane. Successful jug handle navigation is a sure sign that one is from New Jersey.

**The Oranges**
A collective term for the towns of Orange, East Orange, South Orange, and West Orange. Rarely used in reference to colors or to citrus fruit.

# Weird Animal News

*Meet four crazy critters from the Garden State.*

## On the Moooove

In 2014 a brown cow went on a "crime spree" in Morristown: jaywalking in the road, causing near-accidents, and invading private yards and complexes. The cow, named Bessie, had been destined for the slaughterhouse when she managed to break out of her trailer. The police were called to several locations, but Bessie managed to elude them because, according to the police chief, she's a "smart cow." Finally, officers drove behind Bessie to steer her down busy South Street and back to her owner's farm in Harding.

But the story got weirder when a farmhand mentioned, "Oh, by the way, a bull is missing, too." Indeed, Loney the bull was also wandering around Harding after jumping two fences at the same time that Bessie escaped. Though much bigger in size than Bessie, Loney was better at staying incognito. When witnesses spotted him, he fled into the woods. After almost a week on the run, Loney was located near the Garden State Parkway and corralled. Ultimately, both cows got a reprieve—instead of going to slaughter, they were sent to a farm in Wyckoff.

*A brown cow like this one wandered the streets of Morristown in 2014.*

## Honey! There's a Bee in Here!

Fact: It's illegal to kill honeybees in New Jersey. So what do you do if you notice lots of bees making beelines from your garden to the side of your house? You call a bee rescuer. That's what Cape May resident Victoria Clayton did in 2012 when bees swarmed her house, a former bed-and-breakfast dating to the 1860s, through a laundry vent on the third floor. In the attic was a big surprise: *30,000* honeybees. In less than a year, they had built a hive three feet long and dripping with 25 pounds of honey! If the bees were allowed to remain, the historic home "would have eventually had honey dripping from the ceilings and that could have caused dry rot," says Gary G. Schempp, whose rescue business focuses solely on honeybees. The bees in Clayton's house got a sweet deal—they were relocated to Schempp's own apiary.

## What a Nut!

One night in 2011, around 10 p.m., the emergency room at Robert Wood Johnson Hospital in Rahway got a surprise visitor. A grayish-brown flying squirrel caused chaos as it skittered around the ER, dodging patients and workers who trapped it in a trauma room. There, it launched off an 8-foot-high lamp into the glass wall, trying to escape. "It would climb up on a light and would jump off and glide" toward the glass, said fire department captain Ted Padavano. When it fell to the ground, "it would take off like lightning"…and then hit the glass again. It took about ten minutes for two firefighters to wrangle the dazed critter. After throwing a blanket over it and wrapping it up, they released it into the woods. The oddest part? It was the second time in *two weeks* that a flying squirrel had dropped in at the hospital, prompting speculation that squirrels had nested in the building. Maybe hospitals just make 'em squirrelly.

## Twitter Snake

And the award for most popular snake goes to…the Hopatcong Anaconda, which at last count had more than 800 followers on Twitter. How? During the summer of 2014, several residents reported seeing a huge snake in and near Lake Hopatcong. It was described by witnesses (who were clearly not snake experts) as a 10-foot long, or maybe 20-foot long, boa…or python…or anaconda. Photos and video of the snake were too grainy to be helpful, and whenever animal-control officers arrived, there was no snake in sight. To be funny, someone started a Twitter account for the creature. The posts revealed its daily life ("Crap! The dentist says I need braces. My life is ruined."), its pet peeves ("For the record, they're using an old photo of me. That was during my awkward teen phase. How embarrassing."), and its life in hiding ("Watching *Karate Kid*! Nobody knows I'm under this couch. Hopatcong residents have the best taste in movies."). Capitalizing on the snake, the local donut shop introduced "Snake Hopatcong" donuts topped with blue frosting and a gummy worm, and stores began selling "Snake in the Lake" T-shirts.

Meanwhile, animal-control officers enlisted the help of reptile specialist Gerald

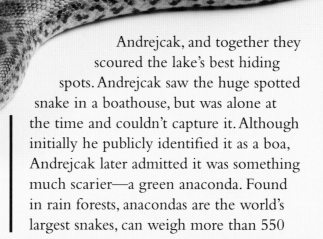

*Anacondas are the largest snakes in the world.*

Andrejcak, and together they scoured the lake's best hiding spots. Andrejcak saw the huge spotted snake in a boathouse, but was alone at the time and couldn't capture it. Although initially he publicly identified it as a boa, Andrejcak later admitted it was something much scarier—a green anaconda. Found in rain forests, anacondas are the world's largest snakes, can weigh more than 550 pounds, and are stealthy hunters in the water. Adrejcak claimed, "I've known its species [since last week], but I was sworn to keep my mouth shut by local officials to avoid causing a panic." How did authorities respond? By discrediting him and calling off the search: They said "there's no credible scientific evidence" of any large snake in the area, and encouraged residents to proceed with life as usual. They also never caught the snake. All clear!

*Lake Hopatcong looks peaceful in this picture, but in 2014, it was home to a terrifying creature.*

# You Light Up My Life

*Our waterways have been used for trade for more than 300 years, and for just as long, ships have had to navigate the tricky coastline. Here are six of the many lighthouses that dot the coastline and have made New Jersey a safer harbor.*

## Absecon

**Location:** Atlantic City
**Built:** 1857
**Height:** 171 feet

This 16-story lighthouse is the tallest in New Jersey, and its light is visible 19 miles out to sea. The first keeper, Daniel Scull, was paid an annual salary of $600 per year. Although not officially used today, Absecon is the only lighthouse that still has its original, first-order Fresnel lens.

*The Cape May Lighthouse keeps watch over the South Jersey shore.*

*The Absecon Lighthouse stands tall in 1900.*

## Cape May

**Location:** Cape May City
**Built:** 1823
**Height:** 157 feet

Some say that the English laid a foundation for this lighthouse in the 1700s, but hard evidence for that has yet to be found. What we do know is that the Cape May lighthouse is the second oldest in the state and has been rebuilt twice—in 1847 because of erosion and in 1859 because of poor construction. This red-roofed lighthouse still serves as a navigational aid. Its 1,000-watt bulb and curved mirrors project a beam of light 24 miles out to sea.

## Barnegat

**Location:** Ocean County
**Built:** 1858
**Height:** 165 feet

Located on the northernmost tip of Long Beach Island, this famous red-and-white landmark used to flash once every ten seconds in every compass direction. Barnegat stopped serving officially in 1927, but it reopened to the public in 1991 after extensive renovations.

*The Twin Lights lighthouse*

## Twin Lights

**Location:** Highlands
**Built:** 1828
**Height:** 40 feet

Originally built in 1828 and rebuilt in 1862, this unique complex has two towers, one octagonal and the other square. Both towers can shine their lights up to 22 nautical miles. In 1841 this lighthouse was the first in the United States to use Fresnel lenses. It also served as the site of the first test of the wireless telegraph by inventor Guglielmo Marconi.

## Sandy Hook

**Location:** Middletown Township
**Built:** 1764
**Height:** 103 feet

The waters leading into New York Harbor can be treacherous, and the Sandy Hook Lighthouse was built to guide trading vessels into the harbor safely. During the American Revolution, loyalist forces occupied the lighthouse while patriots tried but failed to put the light out. The lighthouse was battered again in 2012 when Hurricane Sandy struck the New Jersey coastline, but it came through mostly unscathed; several of the neighboring buildings were damaged, though. Sandy Hook is the oldest lighthouse in New Jersey and the oldest still in use in the United States.

## Hereford Inlet

**Location:** North Wildwood
**Built:** 1874
**Height:** 49.5 feet

Now listed on the National Register of Historic Places, this lighthouse had to be moved inland 150 feet in 1913 after a severe storm damaged its foundation. In 1964 the lights were put out when a skeleton tower took over its job. Luckily, in 1986, they put the lights back on, and now the Coast Guard maintains the site. Visitors can take in the tower and the lovely gardens that surround it.

*Sandy Hook is the oldest lighthouse in New Jersey, dating back before the Revolutionary War.*

# Strange Trip

*Taking a road trip through New Jersey? Make time for detours to these towns—they've got some stops you won't want to miss!*

## Magnolia

Outside Royal Tire and Auto of Magnolia stands a huge Muffler Man—one of several across the country…except this one looks like he's wearing lipstick and pink pants because the sun has faded his colors.

## Mantua

Check out a toothbrush fit for Paul Bunyan—an oversized tooth and toothbrush sit on the lawn of a local dental office.

## Montague

An estate here, dubbed Luna Parc by its eccentric owner, is adorned with brightly colored sculptures, psychedelic mosaics of tile and glass, taxidermied animals, and other weird objects. Tours are by appointment only.

*Dental accoutrememnts in Mantua*

## Newtonville/Buena

In his free time, mechanic William Clark (nicknamed "Robot Man") built robots using old car parts. At various automotive businesses around these towns, you can see his work—including robot musicians, robot animals, a robot with flashing headlights for eyes, and a robo-mother pushing a carriage.

## New Gretna

On Route 9 near Bass River, there's a mansion guarded by giant statues…inside and out. Dinosaurs, water dragons, giraffes, a Transformers robot, a red dragon, a Statue of Liberty, and a Korean warship replica are among the things on display.

## Rio Grande

The one-legged giant outside Menz's Restaurant stands in for original owner Franklin Menz, who lost a leg to diabetes and often greeted customers there.

## Edison

The 130-foot lightbulb tower in Menlo Park is a tribute to inventor Thomas Edison. Built on the site of his old laboratory, the tower has a big, glowing bulb and used to play music (until there were noise complaints).

*Right: The Menlo Park lightbulb tower*

*The colorful Luna Parc*

*Menz's Restaurant's one-legged giant*

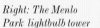

# The Heart of Princeton

*Called the most famous college building in the United States, Princeton University's Nassau Hall also played an important role in colonial history.*

## Situated and Celebrated

Visit Princeton and you can't miss stately old Nassau Hall. Situated in the middle of the campus, this building has been the heart and soul of the university since it was built in 1756. For many students it symbolizes the university itself. Today the building houses mostly administrative offices, but its history is much more colorful and it played an important role in our country's early years.

Before Nassau Hall, the College of New Jersey (as Princeton University was called then—it officially changed its name in 1896)

had convened in the Elizabethtown home of Reverend Jonathan Dickinson, its first president. Then it moved to the First Presbyterian Church in Newark. The college's trustees, however, were uncomfortable with these arrangements because they were concerned that Elizabethtown and Newark were too exciting and students would be distracted from their studies by the temptations of big-city life. They wanted the college situated in a sleepy, bucolic hamlet, far away from temptation. The town of Princeton fit the bill.

*Jonathan Dickinson, Princeton's first university president*

## What's in a Name?

So how did Nassau Hall get its name? The building was almost called Belcher Hall after New Jersey's provincial governor, Jonathan Belcher, a keen supporter of the fledgling college. But Belcher declined the honor and suggested that the building be named instead in memory of "the Glorious King William the Third who was a Branch of the Illustrious House of Nassau." (King William was also known as William of Orange—hence Princeton's school colors, orange and black.) On December 3, 1755, college president Aaron Burr Sr. wrote, "We have begun a building at Princeton which contains a [h]all, library, and rooms to accommodate about one hundred students." When completed in 1756, Nassau Hall was the largest stone structure in the colonies.

For the first 50 years of its existence, the college was housed entirely in Nassau Hall. On its three main floors were a library, a two-story prayer hall, and 42 rooms for classes, offices, and student housing. The

*Princeton University's Nassau Hall in 1903*

*Princeton's school colors (orange and black) were inspired by the British king William of Orange.*

dining hall, kitchen, and steward's quarters were housed in the basement—which later also included additional rooms for students. According to Thomas Jefferson Wertenbaker, a chairman of Princeton's Department of History, "So closely did the building become identified with the college, that for many years it was customary to speak of graduating, not from the College of New Jersey, but from Nassau Hall."

## Bowling for Scholars (and Tutors)

There is little doubt that Princeton's earliest graduates were serious and sober young men. Roused each morning to mandatory

*Princeton students find time for fun.*

prayer by a bell at 5:00 a.m., the students were expected to behave in exemplary fashion and occupy their time with study, discussion, and other scholarly pursuits. They were subject to strict rules of conduct and a rigid pecking order. Even the use of nicknames was forbidden.

But like most college students, Princeton's undergrads were partial to blowing off steam with pranks and practical jokes. In his 1914 book *Princeton*, Varnum Lansing Collins writes of the rambunctious relationship between students and tutors that manifested itself in all-out prank wars. To thwart the efforts of tutors checking up on them, students would build barricades of wood on stairways and entrances to keep them out. Tossing the occasional firecracker out a window startled college authorities—and amused undergraduates to no end. Students would often coax reluctant animals (calves, donkeys, and even horses) to climb to the upper floors of the hall, where authorities had to struggle to get them back down again. But probably the most dangerous source of fun was rolling heated cannonballs down Nassau

Hall's long central corridor. Presumably, any unwary tutor who didn't run away and attempted to stop the noisy projectile would find himself surprised, if not burned, by the hot metal.

## The British Are Coming!

All was not fun and games in colonial Princeton, however, especially as the Revolutionary War brewed around the college. In January 1774, to show their allegiance to the patriots, students stole an entire year's supply of tea and, as the college's bell tolled, used it to fuel a large bonfire in front of Nassau Hall.

John Witherspoon, president of the college at the time of the Revolutionary War, was also a signer of the Declaration of Independence. In November 1776, as the fighting approached Princeton, President Witherspoon sent all the students home. The British took control of Nassau Hall on December 2. For a month, control of the building shuffled back and forth between the British and the Continentals. It was variously used as barracks, a hospital, and a prison for the armies of either side. The British even used the basement for stables. Finally, during the Battle of Princeton, the

Continental army retook Nassau Hall early in the morning of January 3, 1777. American cannons fired two balls at the building. One bounced off the thick exterior stone wall, leaving it pockmarked. Legend has it that the other ball crashed through a window into the prayer room and struck King George II's portrait (some say right in the face). With glee, the Continentals later installed a portrait of George Washington in that very spot, where it remains today.

Both armies proved to have been poor houseguests, and when they finally left, Nassau Hall was a mess. It took about a year for repairs to be completed. The fixes were apparently good enough to allow the building to serve as the nation's capital when the Continental Congress relocated there after fleeing Philadelphia in 1783. From July to November, the Continental Congress met in Nassau Hall's library and used the prayer hall for state occasions.

It was in Nassau Hall that George Washington received the first news of the definitive treaty of peace with Great Britain, which ended the Revolutionary War and recognized the colonies' independence. Among the congressmen who received the good news with Washington were six Nassau Hall alumni.

## Nassau Hall Today

For visitors to Princeton University today, Nassau Hall is one of the top attractions and a main part of the campus tours. On the outside, you can still see the scar on the building's facade made by the British cannonball. It is located on the south wall of the west wing, and the ivy is carefully clipped so that no one can miss it.

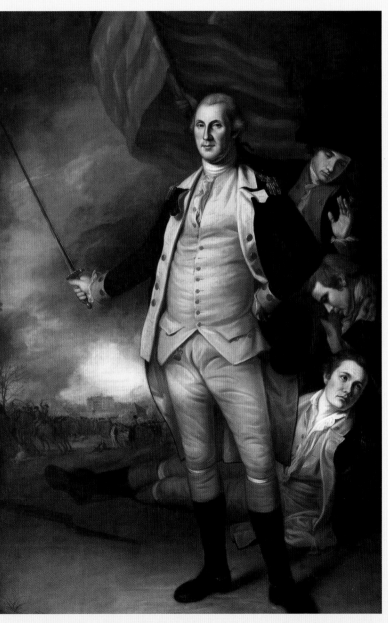

*This portrait of George Washington hangs in Princeton's Nassau Hall.*

# John Basilone

*John Basilone*

New Jersey takes pride in native son and World War II hero, Sergeant John Basilone who grew up in Raritan. In 1940 Basilone joined the U.S. Marines and fought on the Pacific front. During the Battle of Guadalcanal in 1942, Basilone bravely held his battalion together—calming soldiers, repairing equipment, replacing guns, and ensuring that his men had enough ammunition—even if it meant crossing enemy lines to get it to them. Because of his bravery and perseverance, Basilone won the Congressional Medal of Honor. After that, he could have taken a stateside post, but he wanted to return to battle. "I'm a plain soldier. I want to stay one," he said.

On February 19, 1945, the first day of the Battle of Iwo Jima, Basilone was mortally wounded. He was posthumously awarded the Navy Cross and a Purple Heart—thus becoming the only enlisted marine in World War II to win the Medal of Honor, the Navy Cross, and a Purple Heart. Raritan still honors its native son every year with a John Basilone Day parade and a bronze statue of this brave, humble hero.

# Living Large

*New Jersey itself may encompass just 7,417 square miles (only three states in the U.S. are smaller), but it's still got some big-league claims to fame.*

## World's Largest Elephant Building, Margate

Lucy, the world's tallest elephant-shaped building, is located a couple of miles south of Atlantic City. The six-story-tall pachyderm was initially built in 1881 as a real estate office. In her lifetime, Lucy has also been a functional home and neighborhood pub. Her ears are 17 feet long, her body 38 feet long, and her head 16 feet high. Made of sheet tin, the oceanfront elephant is now the only elephant registered as a National Historic Landmark. Today visitors can get a guided tour of her interior.

*Lucy the elephant appears on a 1910 postcard.*

*The Colgate Clock is so large that it can be seen from the Bronx.*

## America's Largest Clock, Jersey City

Fifty feet in diameter, the Colgate Clock was built in 1924, the largest single-faced clock on the face of the earth at the time. Facing Manhattan on the New Jersey waterfront, the clock was a tribute to the Colgate-Palmolive Company, which had been a Jersey City native since the turn of the century. Even though Colgate left Jersey City in 1985, the clock remained. It's been said that you can see its 50-foot-wide face as far away as the Bronx. Its minute hand is taller than a Tyrannosaurus rex, and its hour hand is more than 20 feet long.

## World's Largest Concrete Monument, Jersey City

Despite its name, the Lincoln Park Fountain is not in the town of Lincoln Park. It's in Jersey City—in a park called Lincoln Park. It was built in 1911 by sculptor Pierre J. Cheron, who gave the fountain a 10-year guarantee (which it well outperformed). The spot where the fountain sits used to be a baseball diamond for the city's first baseball league. The 53-foot fountain weighs a total of 365 tons. How much is that? About the weight of 75 rhinoceroses.

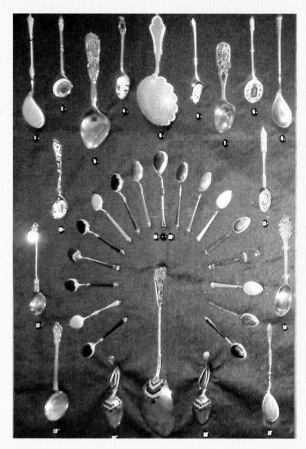

*Some of Bertha Koempel's spoons*

## World's Largest Collection of Spoons, Paterson

Bertha Koempel loved spoons, and she lived when the spoon-collecting craze was at its craziest (1890s–1900s). And collect she did. Visitors to Paterson's historic Lambert Castle can see the fruits of her labors at the Bertha Schaeffer Koempel Spoon Collection. From czarist Russia to your typical spoon-peddling American tourist traps, the collection holds 5,400 collector spoons dating from the 1890s to the 1950s, and includes two of the earliest collectible spoons ever made in the U.S.: one referencing the Salem witch trials and another that includes a portrait of George and Martha Washington.

## World's Largest Model Railroad, Flemington

Like many model-train enthusiasts, Bruce Williams Zaccagnino started a model railway in his basement. But unlike most others, Zaccagnino's hobby grew into what is now the world's largest model railroad. He named his attraction the Northlandz and opened it to the public. Today people can wander through three floors' worth of his exhibit that features more than 100 model trains, 8 miles of track, 50,000 trees, 10,000 freight cars, 400 bridges, and sculpted mountains more than 30 feet tall.

*Above and below: The world's largest model railroad—the Northlandz—winds over mini bridges, through mini mountain passes, and over three floors.*

## World's Largest Pickle Bar, Edison

Harold's New York Deli and Restaurant claims to have the world's largest pickle bar—it's eight feet long with a nice selection of kosher dill, sour, half-sour, and tomato pickles. But the pickle bar isn't the only thing here that's big. The portions at Harold's are huge, too. Pancakes are "monster-size." A foot-high, triple-decker sandwich can easily serve four to six hungry people. A hero sandwich serves at least two. As Harold himself says: "Being that our sandwiches and dinners are of humongous portions, we encourage you to share at no extra charge."

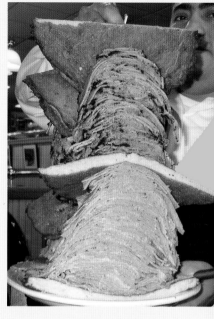

*Harold's Deli in Edison offers foot-high sandwiches.*

# A Sticky Situation

*Saltwater taffy is a favorite boardwalk treat, but it turns out that no one is sure who invented it.*

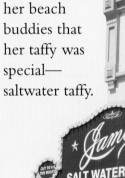

*Kids clamor for saltwater taffy in 1921.*

## From the Mouths of Babes

The most popular origin tale claims that David Bradley, an Atlantic City candy merchant, kept his inventory on a cart on the Boardwalk, which was just a few steps above the sand at that time. One night in the early 1880s, a storm blew in and the waves soaked the cart with—you guessed it—salt water. When a young customer asked for some taffy the next day, Bradley sarcastically told the girl that she must mean the *saltwater taffy*. She bought the candy and later was overheard by both Bradley's mother and his sister telling her beach buddies that her taffy was special— saltwater taffy.

## Sweet Home, NJ

First things first: Belying its name, saltwater taffy contains no salt water. Nor do recipes for the soft, smooth, glossy, airy, chewy, pastel-tinted candy call for any more salt than do recipes for other candies. But those seem to be the only things we know for sure about this candy's sticky story.

It seems that nobody can agree on who, if anybody, can claim his saltwater taffy to be the "original." When this candy was first created is also hotly debated. Less at issue, however, is where. Though some insist that Midwestern county fairs first touted the confection, New Jersey's Atlantic City and its famous boardwalk are generally thought to be its home.

*Enoch James's taffy shop has been around since the late 1800s.*

# Original Salt Water Taffy

PICK YOUR OWN — 16 FLAVORS  $6.29 PER POUND

MINIMUM $1.00 – PLEASE, ASK FOR SAMPLES • PRE-PACKED 1LB. BOXES AVAILABLE $6.29
HAND-PACKED SPECIAL FLAVORS - ADD $.50 PER POUND

*Fralinger's Salt Water Taffy popped up on the Atlantic City Boardwalk in 1885.*

The Bradley women knew a good gimmick when they heard one, and they encouraged David to keep the moniker as a sales tactic. The candy that weathered the storm produced a name that has now weathered more than a century. Bradley ultimately went out of business, though.

## Taffy Wars

Savvy entrepreneur Joseph Fralinger never claimed to be the first to sell the sticky sweets, but he is generally acknowledged as the Saltwater Taffy King. Fralinger started selling the taffy on Atlantic City's Boardwalk in 1885, and his family business is still doing so today.

Soon, however, Enoch James moved to Atlantic City from the Midwest, and Joseph Fralinger had a mighty battle on his hands.

The so-called Taffy Wars between the two men and their companies lasted more than 100 years. A worthy opponent, James was already an experienced candy man (his company's logo says it was "Established 1880"). And some say, though, that he was already making taffy when he relocated his family to the East Coast.

## Making a Federal Case Out of It

By the early 1920s, Fralinger and James had lots of competition: More than 400 others were also making and selling saltwater taffy, and so in 1923, the question of any

one company being able to claim that it was the "original" maker of saltwater taffy went all the way to the Supreme Court. The court declared that taffy was "born of the ocean and summer resorts and other ingredients that are the common property of all men everywhere." Basically, its answer was—in Atlantic City lingo—"no dice." According to the court, too many people had been using the term for too long for one company to claim it was the "original." To this day, both Fralinger and James taffies still use the "O" word on some of their boxes…and they're now both owned by the same company.

# Lights, Camera...Jersey!

*New Jersey and Hollywood: made for each other? You'd be surprised—a number of classic (and some not-so-classic) films have New Jersey as their stomping grounds. Here are a few of our favorites.*

### On the Waterfront (1954)

Marlon Brando was a contender with his gripping performance as Terry Malloy, a former prizefighter turned hood who goes up against a crooked mobster (is there any other kind?) on the docks in Hoboken. The movie filmed on location in Hoboken and included actual local longshoremen as extras. Likely the most honored New Jersey film, *On the Waterfront* won eight Oscars, including Best Actor for Brando, Best Director for Elia Kazan, and Best Picture.

*Marlon Brando looks thoughtful in* On the Waterfront.

*Susan Sarandon and Burt Lancaster share a scene in* Atlantic City.

### Atlantic City (1980)

In this film, Burt Lancaster plays a washed-up numbers runner who is under the impression he used to be more important than he really was. Susan Sarandon is a young woman who dreams of dealing blackjack in the casinos of Monaco. The two of them together make for a bittersweet film about "things that should have been but weren't" and "things that could be but probably won't." Lancaster and Sarandon both notched Oscar nominations for the film.

### Return of the Secaucus 7 (1980)

The debut film of writer/director John Sayles concerns the trials and tribulations of baby boomers coming to grips with the fact that they're getting older and becoming the adults they swore they'd never trust. Sound oddly like *The Big Chill*? Yeah, well, this film was done first and cheaper. It cost only $60,000 to make—Sayles paid for it by writing scripts for cheesy horror flicks like *Piranha*. Sayles returned to New Jersey as a setting for later films such as *Baby It's You* and *City of Hope*; he also directed videos for Bruce Springsteen.

*Robert De Niro (left) and Sylvester Stallone in* Cop Land.

*From left: Actors Peter Sarsgaard, Natalie Portman, and Zach Braff get soaked in a scene from* Garden State.

## Cop Land (1997)

In *Cop Land,* Sylvester Stallone put aside his outer action hero and reconnected with his inner actor. He put on more than 40 pounds (mostly by eating pancakes) to play the beaten-down Sheriff Freddy Heflin, the head cop in a little northern New Jersey town that's home to a large and corrupt group of New York City cops. They belittle Sly's character for being small-town, but when a rookie cop shows up dead, the sheriff is inexorably drawn into the action. Stallone's performance received some solid critical reviews and held its own against a very talented cast, including Robert De Niro, Harvey Keitel, and (New Jerseyan) Ray Liotta.

## Harold & Kumar Go to White Castle (2004)

Two high-achievers, uptight investment banker Harold and

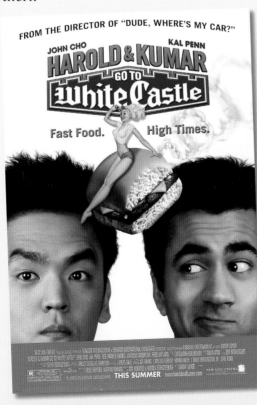

laid-back medical school candidate Kumar, are on a quest. Thanks to some marijuana and the resulting munchies, their mission is to find a 24-hour White Castle to buy some sliders (also known as burgers). This journey into the heart of New Jersey puts our heroes in contact with Princeton students, wife-swappers, extreme-sports freaks, and Neil Patrick Harris as himself. As stoner films go, this one is pretty funny—even if you're not totally baked—and it spawned two sequels: *Harold & Kumar Escape from Guantanamo Bay* (2008) and *A Very Harold & Kumar 3D Christmas* (2011).

## Garden State (2004)

Zach Braff is a TV actor from New Jersey who, in this film he wrote, directed, and stars in, plays—you guessed it—a TV actor from New Jersey. The actor goes home for his mother's funeral, deals with family resentments, meets up with old friends from high school, and meets a really great girl (played by Natalie Portman). This unassuming little film took a lot of folks by surprise with its wit and depth, which of course makes it a perfect New Jersey story—one that gets underestimated and then just sneaks up on you.

# Pirates of the Jersibbean

*Get out your metal detectors—it's time to go treasure hunting.*

*A 17th-century painting shows pirates attacking a British navy ship.*

## Arghhh!

In the old days, there was no need to travel to the Caribbean to find legendary cutthroats like Henry Morgan, Blackbeard, and Captain Kidd. When things got hot for pirates in southern waterways, they put in time in Jersey, where the jagged coastline offered plenty of creeks, inlets, bays, and marshes to hide in. Buccaneers prowled New Jersey waters from the northern tip of Sandy Hook all the way south to Cape May, where they stopped for fresh water. Another popular spot, Ocean Beach, offered a great place to scout approaching merchant ships and launch surprise attacks.

As a matter of fact, pirates were often welcomed in colonial New Jersey. Local politicians and businessmen were happy to protect them…and profit from them. Many wealthy New Jersey colonists invested in pirate expeditions and traded in plundered goods. And three of history's most famous pirates had special ties to New Jersey.

## Henry Morgan

Born in Wales in 1635, Henry Morgan became one of the most successful pirates to sail the high seas. In the 17th century, he made a name for himself by plundering Spanish ships, Cuban cities, the Caribbean, and Central America. Other pirates were hunted or executed, but Morgan used his wealth and highborn relatives to escape capture and become Sir Henry Morgan, governor of Jamaica. In fact, he became so respectable that when he was called a pirate in print, he sued for defamation of character—and won.

Although he's most famous for his exploits in the Caribbean, local legends say that Morgan liked to hang out in New Jersey, where he also had friends and family. The Morgan section of Sayreville is allegedly named for his relatives, who set up their homestead near that favorite pirate hangout, Raritan Bay. Rumor has it that Sir Henry liked to have a drink at the Old Spye Inn, which once stood at the foot of Old Spye Inn Road in Sayreville (it burned down in 1976). But that story is probably just wishful thinking: The inn was likely built around 1703, and Henry Morgan died in 1688.

*This 1887 painting by Howard Pyle depicts pirate Henry Morgan (left) recruiting men to join his band of buccaneers.*

*Edward "Blackbeard" Teach, shown in this 18th-century painting, was one of the most fearsome pirates to sail the seas.*

## Blackbeard

Born in England around 1680 as Edward Teach, Blackbeard came to pirate power in 1717. His colorful nickname accurately described his extravagantly long black beard—sometimes he braided it, tied it up in ribbons, and even stuck flaming pieces of hemp in it. Teach commandeered a French merchantman, turning it into a 40-gun pirate vessel that he named the *Queen Anne's Revenge*. He then launched a reign of terror along the Atlantic seaboard from Maine all the way to Trinidad.

One of Blackbeard's haunts was near Little Egg Harbor in New Jersey. Legends say that he performed one of his impressive escapes from the British navy in the wetlands near Brigantine Beach. While the navy searched, Blackbeard hid underwater in a marsh, breathing through a reed until the coast was clear. In Blackbeard's case, though, the settlers were probably sorry he escaped because not even landlubbers were safe from his thieving cohorts who rowed up the creeks and rivers to attack and plunder farms. In one case, locals in what is now Middletown stood up to Blackbeard—who had raided their town for supplies—engaging his pirates in a fierce battle, refusing to give up their flour and smoked ham without a fight. They prevailed, and the pirates went on to easier pickings.

During his career in crime, the swashbuckler amassed a huge fortune, and according to legend, one stormy night in 1717, he sailed up the Delaware River in Burlington to bury treasure chests near a saloon on what is now Wood Street. Blackbeard shot one of his own men and a huge black dog, burying them both with the treasure to guard it. He never returned to get his loot, but supposedly, the black dog's ghost has remained—prowling Wood Street to defend Blackbeard's stolen booty—which has yet to be found.

*Captain Kidd supervises as pirates bury his treasure in this Howard Pyle painting.*

## Captain Kidd

William Kidd, the son of a minister, was born in Scotland around 1655. By the time he came to New York in the 1690s, he was already a successful privateer. (Privateers were legal pirates who worked for a government—in Kidd's case, the British government authorized him to attack enemy ships in return for a share of the spoils.) Traveling to New York, Kidd married a wealthy widow and, for a time, enjoyed respectability and a high rung on the social ladder.

But in 1696, Kidd's fortunes changed. He left New York on the 34-cannon *Adventure Galley* with aristocratic investors and orders to attack pirates and French ships. He took a ship with French papers, the *Quedagh Merchant*, which carried a cargo worth a fortune (millions in today's currency). But while at sea, he learned that his backers were in political trouble in England and that he was now considered a dangerous pirate with a price on his head. (Some historians claim the Scotsman actually had committed an act of piracy and deserved these charges.)

In 1699 Kidd sailed back to New York proclaiming his innocence and waving his papers showing he was a privateer and not a scurvy pirate. He stopped along the way to bury booty on Gardiners Island near Long Island, New York, and used it as a bargaining chip to get himself off the hook. "A pardon for me, some treasure for you," he told authorities. Alas, the chip didn't work. Kidd was arrested, tried, and hanged in London in 1701. His body hung in an iron cage above the river Thames as a warning to all considering piracy.

Authorities recovered the Gardiners Island treasure, and many believed that they found it all. But some treasure hunters and historians claim that the recovered Gardiners Island booty was only a quarter of Kidd's vast fortunes. They believe that Kidd also sailed along the Jersey Shore and buried much of his treasure there before he returned home to New York. But where could Kidd's treasure be? A beach near Brigantine Inlet is rumored to have treasure from one of Kidd's earlier voyages. Sandy Hook and Cliffwood Beach are two other often-mentioned hot spots. Captain Kidd would probably have anchored at Sandy Hook—popular with smugglers in those days—before his final trip and arrest in New York. It's rumored that he buried three-quarters of his great treasure there in a site marked with pine trees, but those markers are long gone.

Spanish gold coins *have* been found near Cliffwood Beach. Some of those coins were found in a body of water now called Treasure Lake, and visitors to Cliffwood Beach still bring metal detectors to search the area. So far they haven't found a large haul, but hope still exists that some of Kidd's fabulous treasure will eventually be detected.

*A treasure hunter searches the beach for pirate gold.*

# Hometowns: Paterson

*Alexander Hamilton put Paterson on the map...literally.*

## The Stats

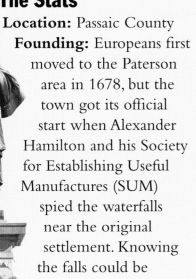

*Alexander Hamilton*

**Location:** Passaic County

**Founding:** Europeans first moved to the Paterson area in 1678, but the town got its official start when Alexander Hamilton and his Society for Establishing Useful Manufactures (SUM) spied the waterfalls near the original settlement. Knowing the falls could be a power source for factories, SUM bought the land and created the first planned industrial community in 1701. The city itself was incorporated in 1831.

**Current Population:** 145,219

**Size:** 8.73 square miles

**What's in a Name?** Paterson is named for New Jersey's resident patriot, William Paterson. He was New Jersey's representative to the 1787 Constitutional Convention, governor of New Jersey, and an associate justice of the Supreme Court.

## Claims to Fame

- Samuel Colt built his first gun factory in Paterson in 1836. They made handguns, rifles, carbines, and revolving shotguns.

*Passaic Falls*

- Passaic Falls, also called the Great Falls, is located in Paterson and is the second-highest waterfall east of the Mississippi. Seventy-seven feet tall and 280 feet wide, this waterfall's energy was harnessed to power local textile, silk, and locomotive industries.

- Nicknamed Silk City, U.S.A., Paterson wove more than 50 percent of the country's silks in 1870.

- Paterson was the birthplace of funnyman Lou Costello. Today there's a life-size statue honoring the comedian. Entitled *Lou's on First*, the bronze figure carries a bat and wears his trademark derby.

- Bob Dylan immortalized the city in his 1975 song "Hurricane," about the infamous boxer Ruben "Hurricane" Carter, accused of four shootings in a Paterson bar in 1966. Convicted in 1967, Carter spent nearly 20 years in prison before a federal court voided his conviction in 1985. His story also inspired a 1999 film called *The Hurricane,* starring Denzel Washington.

*Left: The art for Dylan's 1975 song "Hurricane" featured Carter and garnered public support for his defense.*

*Below: Bob Dylan vists Hurricane Carter in prison.*

# The Genius on Mercer Street

*To his neighbors in Princeton, Albert Einstein was just one of the locals and the embodiment of an absentminded professor. But here's the story behind how this intellectual giant came to live in the Garden State and what happened when he got there.*

## The Road to Jersey

Einstein first visited the United States in 1921, when he accompanied scientist and future Israeli president Chaim Weizmann on a fund-raising trip to benefit the medical school of the Hebrew University in Jerusalem. During the three months Einstein spent here, he gave a series of lectures on relativity at Princeton University (the talk was in German, and translated into English afterward). He was reported as saying, "I also found Princeton fine. A pipe as yet unsmoked. Young and fresh." Apparently the town made quite an impression on him.

In the 1930s, while living and teaching in Berlin, Einstein became keenly aware of his precarious status as a Jew in Germany. "If relativity is proved right," he once said, "the Germans will call me a German, the Swiss will call me a Swiss citizen, and the French will call me a great scientist. If relativity is proved wrong, the French will call me a Swiss, the Swiss will call me a German, and the Germans will call me a Jew." Einstein's theory of relativity, of course, was accepted, and the world acclaimed the man and his work. But many in Germany demeaned his work anyway, calling it "Jewish physics." As the Nazis rose to power, they burned Einstein's treatises and seized his belongings.

So Einstein left Germany in 1932, just before Adolf Hitler took over, and never

*Albert Einstein lectures in Austria, 1921.*

*Albert Einstein poses with his wife Elsa in the 1920s.*

*Einstein's Mercer Street home still stands in Princeton.*

returned. Although many countries offered him asylum, he remembered the little town of Princeton—also the location of the Institute for Advanced Study, whose philosophy of providing a comfortable setting for serious academic research impressed him. Einstein arrived in New Jersey in October 1933 to become the institute's first permanent faculty member.

Albert Einstein brought his second wife, Elsa, her daughter Margot, and his devoted secretary, Helen Dukas, along. They spent their first few weeks in New Jersey at the Peacock Inn before moving to a rented house at 2 Library Place. Eventually they bought a small Victorian home at 112 Mercer Street, about a mile and a half from the institute's campus.

## Lost: One Fuzzy-Haired Genius

Einstein loved his new home. He once described living in Princeton as "banishment to paradise." And his neighbors were fond of him too—especially since the genius next door was down-to-earth. He loved to walk to and from work, greeting neighbors and stopping to talk to children along the way. The trouble was that Einstein also had a knack for getting lost when he went for a walk—even in the most familiar places. Legend has it that the Einsteins painted their front door bright red because Albert regularly failed to recognize his own house. And he frequently appeared at his neighbors' front doors looking sheepish and confused.

Jon Blackwell, writing in the *Trentonian,* recounted how someone once called the dean's office at the Institute for Advanced Study to ask for directions to Einstein's house. When told that this information couldn't be given out, the caller sighed. "This is Albert Einstein," he said. "I got lost walking home from campus."

## Mr. Einstein's Neighborhood

Einstein also enjoyed being around the neighborhood's children and seemed to regard them with a mixture of amusement and fascination. In the summer, the kids provided him with water pistols, and he engaged them in spirited water fights. (He was said to have been an exceptionally good shot.)

The neighborhood kids also quickly figured out that they lived near a genius. One famous story tells of an eight-year-old girl named Adelaide Delong, who rang Einstein's doorbell, a plate of homemade fudge in her hands, asking for help with her math homework. After accepting the chocolate gift and reciprocating with a cookie, Einstein reportedly told her that his helping her wouldn't be fair to the other girls in her class. "She was a very naughty girl," he said years later, recalling the incident. "Do you know she tried to bribe me with candy?"

## Life and Death in New Jersey

Einstein lived in Princeton until he died at age 76 on April 18, 1955. It was typical of Einstein's humility that he left specific instructions that his house not be turned into a museum or shrine. In accordance with his wishes, it has remained a private residence for members of the institute, with no public visitors allowed. He didn't want people "worshipping at his bones," and his will stipulated that his body be cremated and scattered in a secret location.

An autopsy was performed before the cremation. In an act that has been steeped in controversy, the pathologist, Dr. Thomas Harvey, removed Einstein's brain for study. It was sliced into 240 pieces and kept in jars in Harvey's house. ("It looked like any other brain," Harvey said.) In the years that followed, Harvey gave several pieces of the brain to different researchers in California, Alabama, and Ontario. But he remained in charge of most of Einstein's brain until 1998, when he gave what remained of it to the Princeton Medical Center.

*Field Hall at Princeton's Institute for Advanced Study*

# 100,000,000 Bon Jovi Fans Can't Be Wrong

*It's hard to remember a time when Bon Jovi wasn't a household name, but these Jersey boys from Sayreville weren't always the hair metal gods they are now.*

## Starting Out

The story of Bon Jovi the band begins with Bon Jovi the man: Lead singer Jon Bon Jovi—or, as he's known on his birth certificate, John Francis Bongiovi—was born on March 2, 1962, in Perth Amboy, and raised in Sayreville. From an early age Jon was more interested in music than school. By the time he graduated from Sayreville War Memorial High School in 1980, he'd accumulated more than 100 absences. In the eighth grade, he joined his first band, called Raze, and in high school had another band called Atlantic City

Expressway with future Bon Jovi member David Rashbaum (better known as David Bryan).

Jon's first job in the biz wasn't glamorous: he swept floors at New York's Power Station music studio, which was co-owned by his cousin Tony Bongiovi. As he swabbed up after famous musical acts, he also started cutting demo tapes with the musicians using the studio, including members of the E Street Band and Aldo Nova. (Some of these demos later surfaced on a 1997 quickie CD: *1980–1983—Power Station Years*, credited to John Bongiovi.)

It was one of these demos that broke through for him. A catchy rock tune with a hooky synth line, "Runaway" found its way to a New Jersey radio station in 1983, where it was an instant smash. Bon Jovi quickly assembled a full band with Richie Sambora, Tico Torres, David Bryan, and Alec John Such. They signed to Mercury Records, which released the band's self-titled debut album in 1984. "Runaway" performed reasonably well and cracked the Top 40.

## Hair Metal Poster Boys

The band's follow-up, *7800 Fahrenheit* (allegedly named for the temperature at which rock melts), went gold. Most young rockers would be pleased to achieve this level of fame, but Bon Jovi felt that they could be much bigger. So, they organized a plan of attack. First they got together with songwriter Desmond Child and produced more than two dozen poppy, yet still rocking, tunes. Then they played the songs live for New Jersey and New York fans, to find out which ones had "curb appeal"— that is, which ones the kids thought were good. Those songs were the ones that made the next album.

*The band in 1985*

*Right: Jon Bon Jovi (center) and the guys demonstrate the 1980s hair metal phenomenon.*

*Slippery When Wet* (1986) did exactly what Bon Jovi intended. It rocketed the band to superstardom and sold 8 million copies in the United States alone. Two #1 hits, "You Give Love a Bad Name" and "Livin' on a Prayer," became Bon Jovi's anthems. And Jon Bon Jovi's good looks and long hair helped to ensure that his mug and his music were in high rotation on MTV. Hair metal—an amalgam of blistering rock and sugary pop—had found its poster boys.

*Listeners loved the album* New Jersey, *but critics panned it.*

Having established a winning formula, the band stuck with it for the next album, 1988's *New Jersey*. It was a smash with two #1 hits, but the critics were less than impressed. One of the most charitable reviews came from *Rolling Stone* magazine, which noted: "Jon Bon Jovi is brilliant…at what he does. *New Jersey* has all the virtues and drawbacks of a popular record, hitting all the marks yet remaining thoroughly unidiosyncratic." Other, less kind, critics compared it to the toxic dumps the album's namesake was infamous for. Nevertheless, *New Jersey* sold 5 million copies. Bon Jovi wrapped up its tours and then took a break in 1989. At that time, they were the biggest band in the world.

## A Slight Decline

While his band was on hiatus, Jon Bon Jovi branched out into new things. When movie star Emilio Estevez wanted to use the Bon Jovi hit "Dead or Alive" for his 1990 movie *Young Guns II*, Jon offered him a new song instead: the Western-themed "Blaze of Glory." The song provided him with his

*Bon Jovi rocks out during their 2013 tour.*

*Jon Bon Jovi smiles for fans.*

first solo hit, as well as Golden Globe and Oscar nominations for the song (it won the Golden Globe, but missed out on the Oscar).

The band's biggest challenges, however, began in 1991, when Nirvana's *Nevermind* album blasted out of Seattle and the new grunge style all but killed hair metal. Grunge couldn't quite stop Bon Jovi, but it put a dent in the group's superstar status. The band's 1990s albums, *Keep the Faith* and *These Days*, performed well but not to the megaplatinum level of previous efforts. Bassist Alec John Such left the band in 1994 (he went on to run a motorbike shop and manage other bands), and the group took another hiatus in 1996. Jon Bon Jovi kept himself occupied by making movies, beginning with 1996's *Moonlight and Valentino* (in which he played a hunky handyman). He also released a solo album in 1997, which generated little attention.

## It's Their Life!

But you can't keep a good band down, even if in this case "down" means "a base level of popularity and celebrity most musicians would kill for." By 2000 grunge had leveled off, pop was back in, and the band had fine-tuned their music to encompass the fact that their teenage fans from the 1980s now had families but still wanted to rock out in their minivans. The result was the album *Crush*, which featured the massive hit "It's My Life" that referenced both fellow New Jersey native Frank Sinatra and the love-struck teens (Tommy and Gina) from "Livin' on a Prayer." It gave the band and its fans musical continuity from one musical era to the next.

"Livin' on a Prayer" also took on a special emotional resonance after the 9/11 attacks, when Bon Jovi played a slowed-down version of the song, with a gospel choir, at an October 2001 benefit for New Jersey families affected by 9/11. The attacks also served as a theme for the band's 2002 album *Bounce*, whose title track—yet another anthem—told the story of a guy who "takes the hit, but not the fall," a metaphor for the country in an uncertain time.

## "Why Aren't You Dead?"

With their comeback cemented, Bon Jovi continued to tweak their musical legacy and their critics: 2003's *This Left Feels Right* album took some of the band's biggest hits and reimagined them in various ways—"Livin' on a Prayer" as a torch song, for example, and "Dead or Alive" as a loop-filled remix. They also launched sold-out tours in 2008, 2010, and 2013, and continue writing and playing music today.

And if there were any confusion, the band's 2004 box set of previously unreleased tracks stated their greatness right there in the title: *100,000,000 Bon Jovi Fans Can't Be Wrong*. Critics, who never warmed to the band, may ask Bon Jovi the question from the box set's opening track: "Why Aren't You Dead?" The answer is in the rootsy, rocky music of the song itself— Bon Jovi is too catchy, fun, and New Jersey tough to die.

*A man of many talents, Jon Bon Jovi the actor stars with Katherine Heigl in 2011's* New Year's Eve.

# Westfield's Murder Mystery

*In 1971 the quiet town of Westfield was shaken by what happened to the List family. Patriarch John List had disappeared and his family lay dead in their home. It's still one of New Jersey's most notorious murder mysteries, but what exactly had happened?*

## The Mystery

In December 1971 Westfield was a quiet, upscale northern New Jersey suburb that hadn't seen a murder in eight years, so when the Westfield Police Department received a call to check out the List family's Victorian mansion on Hillside Avenue, officers figured it would be a routine call. The Lists were supposedly away visiting a sick relative in North Carolina, but neighbors and friends had grown concerned. For a month there'd been no communication from anyone in the family.

When the police entered the residence through an unlocked window, however, they met with a bizarre discovery. Inside the huge, cold mansion, loud organ music played over an intercom system. And when officers went into the mansion's ballroom, they discovered four bodies: Helen List and her three teenaged children, Patty, John Jr., and Fredrick. Upstairs, Helen's mother-in-law, Alma List, was found dead in her attic apartment. But where was John List, Helen's husband and the children's father? The man of the house was nowhere to be found.

*The List family, c. 1971*

Authorities soon found a note that John List left to his minister, confessing to the murders. On November 9, in between raking leaves and going to the bank, John had used an automatic pistol to shoot and kill his wife, his mother, and his children. The victims had never gone to North Carolina; instead their bodies had been in the unheated house for a month.

Two big questions remained. First, why had John List done it? He was a polite, church-going accountant who'd never had so much as a traffic ticket. Second, where was he? A massive manhunt turned up no trace of him.

## The Killer Next Door

As the community of Westfield tried to come to terms with the murders, neighbors realized how little they'd known about the family in the three-story mansion called Breeze Knoll. Outwardly, the Lists seemed to fit into the community. Helen had made homemaking her career; she liked to cook and collected cookbooks. The List boys played sports, and daughter Patty wanted to be an actress. The kids' grandmother, Alma List, was a pillar of the local Lutheran church. As for John List, he was quiet, hardworking, and the Lutheran Sunday school teacher.

Only after the murders did the people of Westfield learn how much was going wrong inside Breeze Knoll. Brought up by his strict father and domineering mother to be obedient and religious, John List had tried to raise his own family in the same rigid mold. That—to put it mildly—hadn't worked out. His wife was an alcoholic and

*Police officers survey the List family's home.*

suffered both mentally and physically from syphilis, which she'd contracted from her first husband. Sixteen-year-old Patty was in the throes of teenage rebellion. Fifteen-year-old John Jr. was unruly in school; both he and 13-year-old Freddy were ditching their religion classes. Except for his mother, John's family was straying from the path

ordained by the Lutheran church, and John was too mild-mannered to rule with the firmness he thought they needed.

Financial problems were growing, too. By 1971 John List had lost his job and was heading into bankruptcy. Everything in his life was crumbling around him, including his showy house. Once he'd hoped to

renovate Breeze Knoll; now he could barely afford to furnish it and faced foreclosure. Raised to be proud and self-sufficient, List refused to seek counseling or public welfare. So after much consideration and planning, he formed his own solution to his problems: on November 9, 1971, he killed his family and left town to start over.

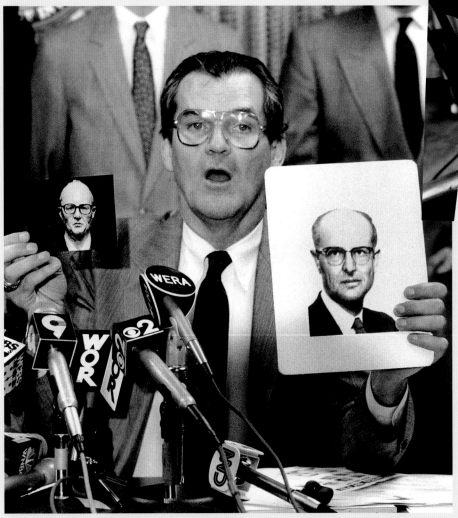

*FBI special agent John McGinley gives a press conference about the hunt for John List in 1989.*

John List was one of the FBI's most wanted.

image out to the public, they reasoned, someone would turn him in. Finally the department turned to a new and popular TV show, *America's Most Wanted*, to help them get their man.

## Vanished!

Police and FBI immediately set up an intensive search for John List, but one week after the bodies were discovered, the authorities admitted that the trail was cold. Having told everyone that the family was leaving town, List had delayed the discovery of the bodies for 28 days. That gave him plenty of time to disappear.

Although police didn't know it then, List had moved to Denver, Colorado, and established a new identity with a phony Social Security number and the alias

Robert P. Clark. A careful, methodical man, List stayed under the radar. He worked as a night-shift cook where his fake ID wasn't scrutinized. Eventually he returned to his profession as an accountant, and he gradually acquired more phony identification, including a driver's license. In 1975 he finally felt safe enough to join a church again. There he met and married his second wife, Delores, who had no idea of his true identity. At the time of his second marriage in 1985, List had been a fugitive for nearly 14 years.

## Down a Cold Trail

But Westfield police never forgot what happened at Breeze Knoll and never closed the case. Detectives were sure that List was still alive—if they could just get his

In 1989, with the trail 18 years cold, *America's Most Wanted* decided to run a show that featured the List case. But since no one had seen List for nearly 20 years, the problem was figuring out what he might look like. They turned to forensic sculptor Frank Bender, asking him to make an "age-progression bust" of the now-64-year-old List. To make the bust, Bender explored every aspect of how List would age. He researched how the neck scar from List's mastoid operation would look over time. List's diet, posture, and likely facial expressions were considered as factors in how his face would change. Bender believed that List would make himself look authoritative behind heavy, thick-framed glasses. He was also certain that List—who used to mow the Breeze Knoll lawn in a suit and tie—would be wearing a suit and tie when found.

When the bust was televised on *America's Most Wanted*, friends of a man named Bob Clark were astounded to see how much he resembled the murderer from New Jersey. The show brought in a tip that Bob Clark had moved from Colorado to Virginia.

*Above: Forensic sculptor Frank Bender (right) discusses his bust of John List with America's Most Wanted host John Walsh in 1989.*

Eleven days later, police tracked him down, and John List was finally arrested for murder.

## The Nation Watches

List was extradited to New Jersey for trial. The nation followed the seven-day event, fascinated by the final mystery of why List had done it. List's attorney, Elijah Miller, used his client's own explanation as part of his defense. List had killed his family to save them. He couldn't support them financially, and he didn't want them to suffer poverty or know the shame of living on welfare. Also, if he killed them before they could reject Christianity (as he believed they soon would), they would all go to heaven. According to the defense, a complicated mental disorder prevented List from seeing any other possibilities or truly understanding the horror of what he'd done.

Prosecutor Eleanor Clark, on the other hand, put together a more monstrous motive. List was a cold-blooded killer who decided to rid himself of his financial and emotional burdens. Clark pointed out that List had carefully plotted his own escape and never turned himself in. He went on with a new life showing neither sorrow nor remorse. The jury agreed with the prosecution and found List guilty—he was sentenced to life in prison.

No one lived in Breeze Knoll after the Lists. In a mysterious act of suspected arson, the house burned down nine months after the murders. Eventually another house was built on the site for new owners.

*John List listens to testimony during his 1990 murder trial.*

*The List home burned down in 1972.*

# Quote Him: The Chairman of the Board

*Hoboken–born Frank Sinatra offers up some homespun wisdom. Pull up a chair and listen.*

## Frank on Women

"Never yawn in front of a lady."

"You treat a lady like a dame, and a dame like a lady."

## Frank on Vices

"Alcohol may be man's worst enemy, but the Bible says love your enemy."

"Fresh air makes me throw up. I can't handle it. I'd rather be around three Denobili cigars blowing in my face all night."

"I feel sorry for people who don't drink. When they wake up in the morning, that's as good as they're going to feel all day."

## Frank on Music

"Whatever else has been said about me personally is unimportant. When I sing, I believe. I'm honest."

"You can be the most artistically perfect performer in the world, but an audience is like a broad—if you're indifferent, Endsville."

"Throughout my career, if I have done anything, I have paid attention to every note and every word I sing—if I respect the song. If I cannot project this to a listener, I fail."

## Frank Gets Philosophical

"I'm like Albert Schweitzer and Bertrand Russell and Albert Einstein in that I have a respect for life—in any form. I believe in nature, in the birds, the sea, the sky, in everything I can see or that there is real evidence for. If these things are what you mean by God, then I believe in God."

"Fear is the enemy of logic. There is no more debilitating, crushing, self-defeating, sickening thing in the world—to an individual or to a nation."

*"You only live once, and the way I live, once is enough."*

## Frank on Frank

"I would like to be remembered as a man who had a wonderful time living life, a man who had good friends, fine family—and I don't think I could ask for anything more than that, actually."

"People often remark that I'm pretty lucky. Luck is only important insofar as getting the chance to sell yourself at the right moment. After that, you've got to have talent and know how to use it."

## Frank on Life and Death

"Stay alive, stay active, and get as much practice as you can."

"Dare to wear the foolish clown face."

"You gotta love livin', baby, 'cause dyin' is a pain in the ass."

"May you live to be 100 and may the last voice you hear be mine."

*Above: Sinatra performs in Washington, D.C., in 1991.*

*Left: Frank Sinatra in Hollywood in the mid-1950s.*

# All Aboard!

*Everybody loves a comeback, and the story behind New Jersey's official tall ship is a good one. Once abandoned by its owners and left to rot in the tidal flats of a river, the now tall and stately A. J. Meerwald, a Delaware Bay oyster schooner, has come a long way.*

## Humble Beginnings

When Augustus Joseph Meerwald commissioned a ship in 1928, building a state symbol was the furthest thing from his mind. He just wanted an oyster dredge to expand his two-ship fleet. The oyster business was booming along the Delaware Bay coast in New Jersey, and Meerwald wanted his business to grow along with it. Being a working boat, it was anything but glamorous, but hopefully it would be profitable.

The ship was built in Dorchester, a shipbuilding center on the Maurice River in southern Cumberland County. The 112-foot *Meerwald* had no topmasts. Like most Dorchester ships, its sturdy construction of oak planks on oak frames made it a fine example of the hardworking schooners that were built specifically for sailing the shallows of inland and bay waters to harvest oysters.

*Above: Shucking oysters in Bivalve in 1938.*
*Below: Oyster shells pile up.*

*A New Jersey oysterman steers a boat in 1938.*

*A sign advertises the restored A. J. Meerwald. The restoration roject took eight years.*

*The A. J. Meerwald takes to the sea.*

## Out of the Oyster Biz

Like so many hardworking Americans, the *A. J. Meerwald* was called upon to serve its country in 1942 during World War II. Under the War Powers Act, the U.S. Maritime Commission drafted the schooner to help the U.S. Coast Guard. During its stint in the armed services, most of the *Meerwald*'s sails were removed in order to turn the oyster dredge into a fireboat.

When the war ended, the ship was sold to a businessman who put it back to work in the oyster business. In 1957, though, a parasite wiped out the New Jersey oyster industry, killing an estimated 90 to 95 percent of the critters that year. So in 1959 the old ship was sold again and transitioned to surf clamming. Finally, in the 1970s, the *Meerwald* was retired and abandoned by her owners.

## A Schooner Is Saved

Luckily for the *A. J. Meerwald*, the Delaware Bay Schooner Project rescued the ship and restored it to its former glory. The eight-year, $1 million restoration used only historically authentic materials such as canvas sails, hemp ropes, and cedar planks for the deck. The ship's dock, however, was made from recycled milk and beverage containers because the grayish-brownish composite is resistant to rot and stronger than wood. Another plus, the Cumberland County Improvement Authority estimated that the dock kept more than 240,000 milk jugs out of landfills.

The ship took to the water again in 1996 and has since become a floating classroom where both young and old can learn about the history, natural environment, and local culture along the Delaware Bay. Now docked at the project's headquarters in Bivalve, the ship is available for public sails and schooner day camps, in addition to making the occasional appearance in tall-ship parades and schooner races.

An important symbol of New Jersey's past, the *Meerwald* has a place on both the National Register of Historic Places and the state register. In 1998 New Jersey recognized the *A. J. Meerwald* as its official tall ship.

# Open for Business

*New Jersey is the undisputed Diner Capital of the World—it has more diners than any other state. Here's Uncle John's guide to some of these American icons.*

## What Is a Diner, Anyway?

Depends on whom you ask, but according to the American Diner Museum in Rhode Island, it's a prefabricated restaurant made in one place and shipped to another place for business. Typically diners are fitted with stools and counters and offer reasonably priced food, including breakfast served anytime. From there, the definition gets a little fuzzy. Some are shiny-hulled prefabricated railcars; others are retrofitted trolleys. Many have a 1950s retro theme. Most have a jukebox. Some are even in strip malls. But two things are for certain: they're all American, and they're all over New Jersey.

## Why New Jersey?

Diners began in New England as horse-drawn "night lunch wagons," from which people sold meals to workers on night shifts when everything else was closed. New Jersey took that idea and ran with it. One of the earliest diners came from Jerry Mahoney of Bayonne, the patriarch of the 24-hour pancake house and the New Jersey diner king of his day.

From a horse-drawn carriage in the early 1900s, Mahoney began selling meals like pork and beans and corned beef. By the time the Great Depression rolled around, he'd built quite a business manufacturing railcar-like restaurants (dining by rail back then was a classy affair, so the train theme made the experience more special). Mahoney's diners became a dependable way to get a cheap meal, and he started shipping his railcar diners all over the country—he even offered financing, and eventually took his company public.

But Mahoney didn't do it alone. Many manufacturers cranked out prefab food cafés up and down the East Coast. New Jersey entrepreneurs just did what they do best—tried to make more of them than anyone else. Plus, the abundance of highways makes New Jersey a mobile state, perfect for the proliferation of travel-friendly fare. During the 1950s, the combination of an economic boom and a population boom in the Northeast made an inexpensive cup of coffee and a quick slice of meatloaf or apple pie a hot prospect in the Garden State.

Today, there are more than 500 diners in New Jersey—from die-hard prefab originals to fancy franchises. Listing them all (in one sitting) is impossible. But here are some that are well worth their saltines.

## Bendix Diner (Hasbrouck Heights)

It's hard to imagine a more dinery-looking diner than this one. This art deco–style diner was built in 1947 and has become a Jersey legend for its quality and simplicity, with no apparent plans to go upscale and start serving tapas. From the Formica counter to the big neon lettering, this place looks so much like a typical diner that Hollywood types love to film there (it was even the backdrop for the 1982 movie *Diner*).

*Below: The Bendix Diner has been welcoming hungry travelers since the 1940s.*

## Tick-Tock Diner (Clifton)

If cholesterol is the base of your food pyramid, there's no better place to visit than the Tick-Tock Diner. Its original 1940s facade comes complete with a neon clock and the mantra "Eat Heavy." All the standard diner fare is accounted for, and it's all good. From Greek salad to Belgian waffles, there's decadence for everyone—plus portions are so huge they often get mentioned in first-year macroeconomics courses at Rutgers.

## Miss America Diner (Jersey City)

Americana expert Peter Genovese called this "the best diner in New Jersey," adding that there wasn't even a runner-up. The Miss America got its name when a German immigrant bought this 1950s model and wanted to use the name to declare his patriotism. With its bold neon and stainless steel, the Miss America has become a Jersey City landmark—people come from all around to stake their claims along the Formica for the good food and good coffee.

## Summit Diner (Summit)

As soon as you sit down, you know this is the real deal. The Summit Diner is a down-to-earth eatery with classic diner aesthetics: a small, silver railcar with a counter, stools, and eight prefabricated booths (which, on some mornings, you have to stake out early because they fill up fast). The food is cheap enough for college students, but good enough for students of classic American cuisine. And breakfast is the Summit's high point: big, fluffy pancakes, classic omelets made fast and to order, and coffee that's still actually coffee-flavored. It's been in business since it rolled into town in 1938 and is an official historical landmark.

*The Summit Diner (shown here in 2007) has maintained its classic look.*

# The Lindbergh Baby, Part I

*In 1932 famed aviator Charles Lindbergh's young son, Charles Jr., was kidnapped from his bedroom in Hopewell. The mystery and criminal investigation riveted attention on New Jersey as millions hoped the boy would be found and the kidnapper brought to justice.*

## The Price of Fame

When Charles Lindbergh moved to Hopewell Township, New Jersey, he was a reclusive man—who just happened to be an American hero. On May 20, 1927, Lindbergh had successfully completed a solo, nonstop flight of 33½ hours from New York to Paris in his single-engine plane, the *Spirit of St. Louis*. Lindbergh was the first person to fly nonstop over the Atlantic Ocean, an accomplishment that made him famous. In 1929 he married an equally shy New Jersey heiress and poet, Anne Morrow. The next year their son, Charles A. Lindbergh Jr. (whom the public nicknamed the Eaglet), was born. The media couldn't get enough of the happy family.

The couple lived quietly on the Morrow estate in Englewood, but found it difficult

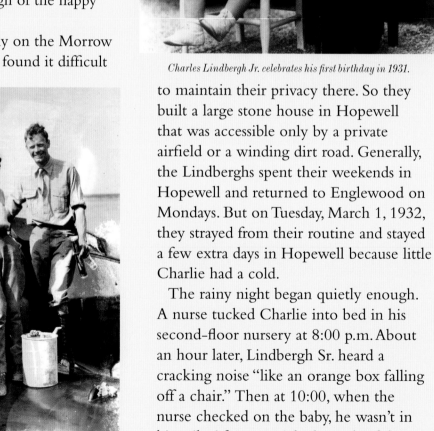

*Charles Lindbergh Jr. celebrates his first birthday in 1931.*

to maintain their privacy there. So they built a large stone house in Hopewell that was accessible only by a private airfield or a winding dirt road. Generally, the Lindberghs spent their weekends in Hopewell and returned to Englewood on Mondays. But on Tuesday, March 1, 1932, they strayed from their routine and stayed a few extra days in Hopewell because little Charlie had a cold.

The rainy night began quietly enough. A nurse tucked Charlie into bed in his second-floor nursery at 8:00 p.m. About an hour later, Lindbergh Sr. heard a cracking noise "like an orange box falling off a chair." Then at 10:00, when the nurse checked on the baby, he wasn't in his crib. After a panicked search of the estate, Lindbergh called the New Jersey State Police in Trenton to report that his son had been kidnapped.

*Charles Lindbergh poses with his famous plane.*

*Anne Morrow and Charles Lindbergh in 1931*

Above: A crime scene photo shows the Lindberghs' Hopewell house and a ladder to the second floor.

Right: A police detective examines sections of the ladder found at the Lindbergh home.

## Media Madness

A happy Lindbergh family had been news, but their tragedy was, as journalist H. L. Mencken put it, "the biggest story since the Resurrection." The crime made headlines around the world, with top billing on radio and in newsreels. Posters of little Charlie's blond dimpled image were everywhere. Police and FBI agents joined in the hunt as tips and Charlie sightings poured in from Michigan to Mexico.

Thousands volunteered to help Lindbergh find his son. Al Capone himself declared that if he were freed from his Chicago jail cell, his underworld contacts could return the child immediately.

One of the many people offering help to the Lindberghs was Dr. John "Jafsie" Condon, a retired principal living in the Bronx. Jafsie often wrote letters to the *Bronx Home News* when he was indignant. And the kidnapping upset him so much that, like thousands of others, he declared himself willing to negotiate with the kidnapper. Amazingly, Jafsie received a letter accepting his mediation offer—a letter marked with the distinctive punched-circle design.

As head of the New Jersey State Police, Colonel H. Norman Schwarzkopf (whose son General H. Norman Schwarzkopf Jr. became famous during the 1991 Gulf War) was officially in charge of the kidnapping investigation. In reality, Schwarzkopf was in awe of the heroic aviator, and it was

## Clues and the Clueless

When the police arrived, they found a chisel and a broken, handmade extension ladder outside the house. Footprints in the muddy ground led away from the structure. But the biggest clue of all was in the nursery, where Lindbergh discovered a note. It read, in part: "Have 50,000$ redy. . .After 2–4 days we will inform you were to deliver the Mony. We warn you for making anything public or for notify the polise the child is in gute care." The note's signature—shaded red circles with three holes punched in the design—would be the signature on all correspondence from the kidnapper.

Unfortunately, police found no fingerprints on the note, and by the next morning, news of the crime had gone public. Twisting roads or not, reporters and gawkers trampled the Lindbergh estate, destroying evidence. Police had not taken casts of the footprints—the throngs ruined the chance to cast them and to look for more evidence outside the house.

Baby Charlie's kidnappers left behind this handwritten note.

Lindbergh who ran things…and agreed to do whatever the kidnapper wanted. Over police objections, Lindbergh authorized the inexperienced, self-promoting (and, some said, suspicious) Jafsie Condon to negotiate on his behalf. Condon received more letters from the kidnapper—who, to prove he had the baby, also sent along Charlie's pajamas. Following the kidnapper's orders, Condon went to a Bronx cemetery on April 2, 1932, and with Lindbergh nearby, he delivered $50,000 in gold certificates to a man with a foreign accent—a man he nicknamed Cemetery John.

## The Eaglet Falls

For all that cash, Condon received only another letter that claimed little Charlie was alive on a boat called the *Nellie*. A search ensued, and Lindbergh flew for days over the coast, but the *Nellie* was never spotted. Then came the horrible news.

On May 12, a Trenton truck driver stopped about four miles from the Lindbergh home, went into the woods to relieve himself, and stumbled over the remains of a toddler. The body was later identified as Charles Lindbergh Jr. The coroner deduced from the condition

of the body that the baby had been lying in the woods since the time of the kidnapping. He died from a blow to the head. Cemetery John had lied and disappeared with Lindbergh's money.

## The Investigation Continues

As the Lindbergh family mourned, the public clamored for quick justice. But the investigation dragged on for two years as investigators pursued suspects and clues that didn't solve the mystery. A few of them were…

# WANTED
### INFORMATION AS TO THE WHEREABOUTS OF
# CHAS. A. LINDBERGH, Jr.
#### OF HOPEWELL, N. J.
## SON OF COL. CHAS. A. LINDBERGH
**World-Famous Aviator**
This child was kidnaped from his home in Hopewell, N. J., between 8 and 10 p. m. on Tuesday, March 1, 1932.

**DESCRIPTION:**

Age, 20 months — Hair, blond, curly
Weight, 27 to 30 lbs. — Eyes, dark blue
Height, 29 inches — Complexion, light
Deep dimple in center of chin
Dressed in one-piece coverall night suit

ADDRESS ALL COMMUNICATIONS TO
COL. H. N. SCHWARZKOPF, TRENTON, N. J., or
COL. CHAS. A. LINDBERGH, HOPEWELL, N. J.
ALL COMMUNICATIONS WILL BE TREATED IN CONFIDENCE
COL. H. NORMAN SCHWARZKOPF
Supt. New Jersey State Police, Trenton, N. J.
March 11, 1932

## L'ILLUSTRÉ
DU PETIT JOURNAL
GRAND HEBDOMADAIRE POUR TOUS

L'ENFANT DE LINDBERGH ENLEVÉ PAR LES GANG

*Left: Charlie's kidnapper was one of America's most wanted criminals.*

*Immediate left and below: The Lindbergh kidnapping was dubbed the "crime of the century," and the story became front-page news all over the world.*

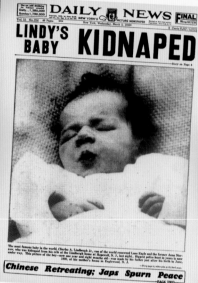

DAILY NEWS FINAL
LINDY'S BABY KIDNAPED

**Chinese Retreating; Japs Spurn Peace**

- **Suspect:** Jafsie Condon. Although Lindbergh continued to support Condon, the police didn't trust him. They questioned him, searched his property, and tapped his phone in an attempt to discover if the old man was actually in league with Cemetery John. Finally they decided Condon was an eccentric but likely innocent.

- **Suspects:** Lindbergh's staff. How did the kidnapper know the Lindberghs were in Hopewell? Or where the baby slept? Cops questioned all insiders, particularly Violet Sharpe, a maid who refused to verify her alibi. Sharpe eventually committed suicide, but it turned out her alibi was solid: the night of the kidnapping, she had gone to a speakeasy with a man who wasn't her fiancé.

*Hauptmann stands trial for Charlie's kidnapping and murder.*

*Above: Bruno Richard Hauptmann (center) is arrested.*
*Left: Colonel H. Norman Schwarzkopf*

- **Clue:** The money. The serial numbers on the gold notes paid to Cemetery John were all recorded and the numbers given to banks. In May 1933, some of that money was turned in to the Federal Reserve Bank in New York City. The deposit slip for the exchange of the currency was signed by J. J. Faulkner—who was never found.

## An Arresting Development

Finally, on September 15, 1934, the cops got a break thanks to an attendant at a Bronx gas station. After a customer paid with a gold certificate that the attendant thought might be counterfeit, he wrote down the customer's license plate number and called police. The cops checked the serial number on the certificate and recognized it as part of the Lindbergh ransom. The customer's license plate ultimately led authorities to Bruno Richard Hauptmann, a 35-year-old carpenter from Germany.

Hauptmann was an illegal immigrant whose description was said to match that of Cemetery John. When police arrested him they found a Lindbergh ransom bill in Hauptmann's wallet and more than $11,000 in ransom money stashed in a tin can hidden in his garage. Authorities were sure they had their man, but Hauptmann and his wife insisted they'd been together at home on March 1. No matter. The stage was set for what would become known as the Trial of the Century.

*Turn to page 128 for the second part of the story.*

# Can It!

*Canned soup has become so common that the cans themselves are now old news. But those cans pack a lot of history. From Maine to mainland China, consumers of soup take a little piece of New Jersey innovation into their pantries every day.*

## Yes, We Can!

The food-processing industry in New Jersey generates around $9.6 billion in sales per year—enough to buy more than 12 *billion* cans of Campbell's Cream of Mushroom Soup. And canned goods make up a big chunk of that cash. French chef Nicolas Appert invented the process of heating and preserving food in jars. And Englishman Peter Durand patented the first tin can. But it was in New Jersey that the practice of food canning really came into its own. It all took off during the Civil War.

Canning existed in the early 1800s but hadn't been perfected. Early canisters (as they were called then) were made by hand

*Union soldiers like these relied on New Jersey's canned tomatoes during the Civil War.*

in a painstaking process of cutting sheets of tin with circular scissors and then soldering them together. A factory could make only about 60 cans a day. The process improved in the 1830s and 1840s, after Englishman

Henry Evans patented a can-making machine. As similar technology spread, New Jersey canneries were soon cranking out thousands of cans per week.

But the foundation for New Jersey's canning claim to fame would be laid in 1847 when Harrison Crosby of Jamesburg had the bright idea to start canning locally grown tomatoes. During the Civil War, these New Jersey tomato canneries kept Union soldiers fed across the nation. And when the war ended, New Jersey kept cranking out the cans—this time to civilians who'd grown a taste for them on both sides of the Mason-Dixon Line.

*The Campbell's world headquarters has been located in Camden since 1869.*

## Campbell's Condenses

In 1869 Joseph Campbell of Camden decided to try his hand at canning vegetables. After a few years of experimentation, he formed Joseph Campbell & Company in 1876, along with a business partner, Abraham Anderson. He canned everything from mincemeat to jellies, but Campbell's first big seller was his canned beefsteak tomatoes—notable because a single tomato filled an entire can.

Then in 1897, one of the managers at Cambell's company, Arthur Dorrance, hired his nephew, a chemist named Dr. John T. Dorrance. John devised a way of condensing soups that would slash shipping costs and lower prices. Because of this innovation, Campbell's just-add-water soups could be sold for only a dime (rather than 30¢), and consumers ate it up—literally. The original Campbell's flavors were chicken, vegetable, consomme, oxtail, and—of course—tomato.

To spread the word, Campbell's began advertising. The company sold dozens of types of soups and soon created an empire—as well as a market for lots of cans. In 1900 the soups took a medal at the Paris Exposition; that's the little gold seal you still see on the can today. By 1922 the soups had become so popular that the company changed its name—it officially became the Campbell's Soup Company.

After more than 100 years of Campbell's soup making, 90 percent of American households stock 11 cans of Campbell's soup in their pantries at all times. With more than 100 million households in the United States, that adds up to over a billion cans of New Jersey heritage around the nation at all times. Campbell's is still headquartered in Camden, and the once one-tomato-in-a-can outfit now sells around a billion dollars' worth of soup every three months.

*Mom makes Campbell's soup in a 1950s ad.*

# North and South

*To misidentify the region from which a Jerseyan hails could be a serious faux pas. So here are a few things to keep in mind when traveling throughout the Garden State.*

## Room with a View or Room to Move?

New Jersey is the fourth-smallest state, but it has the ninth-largest population, making it the most densely populated state in the nation. More than 40 percent of New Jersey's 8.4 million residents have squeezed into the five counties that surround New York City: Bergen, Essex, Hudson, Middlesex, and Passaic. These make up the bulk of the North Jerseyans. By comparison, the five largest counties in the southern part of the state (Atlantic, Burlington, Cape May, Cumberland, and Ocean) house just 1.5 million residents in four times the space. These are the South Jerseyans. There is also a rarely acknowledged group: the Central Jerseyans, hailing from the midsection of the state around Mercer, Middlesex, and Monmouth Counties. But people in this group tend to blend in with their neighbors closest to the south or north.

There is no physical line of demarcation, but Jerseyans know which side they're on. How? By their TV channels. Those north and east of Trenton look to the Big Apple for their news, while the rest find Philly broadcasters on their screens.

*Tourists catch some rays on a North Jersey beach.*

## Dialects

When confronted with a Jerseyan, the most obvious distinction is his or her accent. The popular idea of a North Jersey accent comes from *The Sopranos* ("Fuhgeddaboutit!"), but the Northern accent can be subtler in the real world. Listen for short As—that's what gives the North Jerseyans away. For instance, if you go to a park and hear someone "cawl" his "dawg" and throw it a "bawl," he's probably from the northern half of the state.

A South Jerseyan twang reflects the

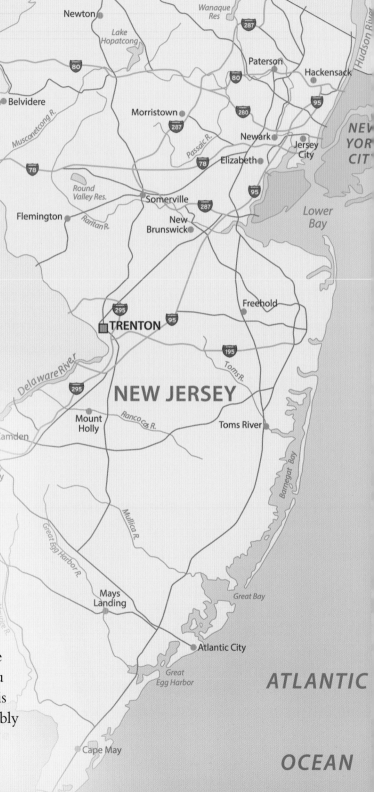

*Giants fans fill MetLife Stadium.*

region's slightly slower pace of life. Words can be lengthened and sometimes have an extra syllable: For example, you may say "home," but they say "hoe-m." Other giveaways: It's not a creek, but a "crick." "On the road" becomes "onna road." If you hear the term "wooder," which means water, you've got a South Jerseyan on your hands.

Slang across both regions can be similar. For example, both groups take their summer vacations "down the Shore," although they flock to different areas:

North Jerseyans tend to gather at the beaches from Belmar to Seaside Heights. South Jerseyans favor Long Beach Island, Avalon, Stone Harbor, and Cape May.

## Divided Sports Loyalties

Long-suffering Jersey sports fans often have little choice but to pledge allegiance to teams from either New York or Philadelphia. Both the Jets and the Giants play at

*The New Jersey Devils are ready for game time.*

*Vintage postcards show off South Jersey's attractions (above) and the beach in Belmar (right).*

MetLife Stadium in East Rutherford but call New York home, in name at least. Only the New Jersey Devils admit to where they live. As a result, New Jersey sports allegiances tend to favor the big city the fans live closest to: North Jerseyans generally like the New York teams, and South Jerseyans prefer the Philadelphia ones.

# Hometowns: Middletown

*Not surprisingly, Middletown occupies a central place in New Jersey's history.*

## The Stats

**Location:** Monmouth County
**Founded:** 1664
**Current Population:** 66,327
**Size:** 41.11 square miles
**What's in a Name?** From the sounds of it, you would guess that Middletown is in the middle of something, right? Well, it was. When the English began to settle the area in the 1660s, they established three villages: Portland Point, Shrewsbury, and Middletown, which was located in between the other two.

## Claims to Fame

- During the American Revolution, most of Middletown remained loyal to the British, which is probably why the redcoats felt safe retreating through the region. Today there are signs along local roads showing their retreat path after the Battle of Monmouth.

- Wealthy Avenue sounds like a place where Middletown's rich and famous might live, but that isn't necessarily so. Despite the haughty moniker, Wealthy Avenue's name comes from something much more humble. Wealthy is a variety of apple (developed around 1860), and the land near Wealthy Avenue used to be an orchard. Other streets—Apple and Baldwin (another varietal)—also reflect the apple's legacy in Middletown.

- The Evil Clown of Middletown has towered over Route 35 since 1956, when it was installed as a mascot for the Food Circus grocery store. Today, the 20-foot-tall sneering clown stands outside a liquor store. He has a real name (Calico) and his own Facebook and Twitter accounts. He even appeared in the 2006 film *Clerks II*.

*The evil clown of Middletown*

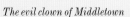

106

# Atlantic City's Own Miss America

*She's smart, talented, pretty, and socially conscious, but Miss America's best assets may be her ability to go with the flow and change with the times.*

Left: A cameraman films Miss America contestants as they walk along the beach in Atlantic City in 1939.

Right: Lois Delander, Miss America 1927, shows off her patriotic costume.

## A Good Gimmick

There she is, Miss America…" For a quarter of a century, host Bert Parks sang that song while a newly chosen Miss America walked down the runway. The song, a crown, and tears of happiness are all part of the pageant, which has been loved, protested, mocked, and imitated for more than 85 years. Miss America may be an American institution, but she's a Jersey girl by birth. The pageant got started in Atlantic City, where it was invented to sell hotel rooms, hot dogs, and taffy.

*The very first Miss America, Margaret Gorman (1921)*

Profits for boardwalk businesses had fallen off in 1921, so the Businessmen's League of Atlantic City went in search of a gimmick to bring crowds in after Labor Day. Their idea? Beautiful girls in a bathing beauty contest!

By the first week of September, Atlantic City held a competition for girls from different cities for a crowd of about 100,000. By 1925 the pageant was receiving radio coverage. And in the 1940s, millions of moviegoers watched Miss America crowned in newsreels before their favorite films. Then, in the 1950s, Miss America went national. Every state was represented by a contestant, and the entire show was watched by millions on TV. Today the contest is one of the longest-running live broadcast events on television. So how has Miss America managed to stay around for so long?

## Making "Judge"ments

One secret of the pageant's success has been its ability to change the rules to emphasize talents other than looking good in a swimsuit:

- Newspapers picked the contestants in the early days; they sponsored photographic popularity contests and sent the winners to Atlantic City. Today's contestants compete in a network of state and local competitions before they can qualify for Miss America.

- In 1935, as a way to improve the pageant's public image, the pageant added a talent segment to the competition. Some of the more interesting "talents" included trampoline bouncing and trained pigeon acts.

- In 1947 scholarships became a big part of the pageant. To show that beauties could also be brainy, an official fourth category called Intellect and Personality (based on judges' interviews) was added.

- Finally, 1989 was the first year of Miss America's "official platform," when each contestant was required to offer a commitment to service on an important social issue, such as increasing literacy, raising awareness of diabetes, or bringing attention to the problems of homeless veterans.

## Prizes! Prizes! Prizes!

As the contest got bigger, so did the prizes:

- Margaret Gorman, the first pageant winner, took home $100 and a golden mermaid statue in 1921.

- In 1925 Fay Lanphier won a starring role in a Hollywood film from Paramount Pictures, *The American Venus*, which featured the pageant as a backdrop. Unfortunately, the movie flopped at the box office.

*Fay Lanphier (above and left) won a role in Hollywood movie as part of her 1925 prize package.*

*Norma Smallwood*

- There was more excitement in 1937 when the newly crowned Miss America, Bette Cooper (from New Jersey), disappeared with her male chaperone in the middle of the night. Romantic rumors flew during a statewide police search. In reality, Cooper had decided to give up the beauty queen life, and her chaperone had taken her home.

- The 1950 winner, Yolande Betbeze, declared she was no "pinup" and refused to wear bathing suits at appearances. The offended sponsor, Catalina swimwear, left the pageant and founded the Miss USA and Miss Universe contests.

*Mary Ann Mobley's 1959 striptease inspired a rule change.*

- In 1926 Norma Smallwood shrewdly used her status as Miss America to earn $100,000 in appearance fees, making her income higher than either Babe Ruth's or President Calvin Coolidge's.

- In 1945 Bess Myerson received the first scholarship award of $5,000. Almost 70 years later, Nina Davuluri, Miss America 2014, received $50,000 in scholarship money.

## Scandalous!

Scandals have also plagued the contest since its early days:

- In 1925 Howard Christy, a contest judge, unveiled a nude statue of Fay Lanphier, the current Miss America. He called his work *Miss America 1925*. Christy later admitted Lanphier never posed for him, but the public remained shocked.

*Yolande Betbeze*

- The talent contest took on a more adult tone when Mary Ann Mobley performed a mock striptease in 1959. She wore a gown, sang the start of an aria, and then did a "wholesome" striptease down to a pair of shorts and a slip, while grinding out "There'll Be Some Changes Made." She won, but "wholesome stripping" was later banned from the contest.

- In July 1984 nude photos surfaced of the winner, Vanessa Williams. They were published in *Penthouse* magazine, and the pageant forced Williams to resign. The title then went to the runner-up, New Jersey's Suzette Charles, who became the second African American and the second Miss New Jersey to wear the crown. Williams went on to release several number-one singles and star on TV shows such as *Ugly Betty* and *Desperate Housewives*.

*Suzette Charles, Miss America 1984, poses with host Gary Collins.*

# A Good State for Sports

*Despite not having many professional sports teams now, New Jersey was once a hotbed for sports and their development. A lot of important athletic firsts occurred in the Garden State.*

*A vintage soccer ball*

## The First Football Game

On November 6, 1869, students from Queen's College (now Rutgers) and the College of New Jersey (now Princeton) played the first college football game. The rules were a little different then, and the game more resembled soccer. Each team had 25 players who wore no pads, helmets, or any other protective gear. Touchdowns were worth only one point and were scored each time a player passed the opponent's goal line. Rutgers won the first match 6–4. In the less famous rematch the following week, Princeton won 8–0. The two teams wanted to play again, but the schools' administrations canceled the game because they thought football was too distracting and took the players away from their studies.

## America's First International Soccer Match

British immigrants founded the first U.S. soccer governing body, the American Football Association (AFA), in Newark in 1884. The AFA team played the first international match between the United States and Canada on Clark Field in what was then Kearny—Canada won, 1–0 (the U.S. won the rematch in 1886). In 1885 the AFA also established the first national championship, which was won by a team from Kearny. Sponsored by the Clark Thread Company (which also employed a lot of soccer-playing Scottish immigrants), the team was called ONT, which stood for Our New Thread.

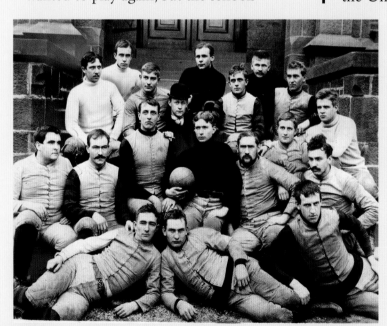

*Left: The Rutgers football team in 1891. The school played in America's first football game in 1869.*

*Right: Harry Holden, captain of the Canadian team that won the first international soccer match in 1885, stands beside his trophy.*

*Left: The Princeton baseball team in 1901*

THE AMERICAN NATIONAL GAME OF BASE BALL.

*Right: A postcard shows a baseball game at Elysian Fields in 1866.*

## The First Professional Basketball Game

The first professional basketball game was played in Trenton in 1898—when the game looked a whole lot different. Players wore velvet shorts, long tights, knee pads, elbow pads, and shin guards. Surrounding the court was a chicken-wire cage that protected the players from fans who often tried to poke them with hat pins and cigarettes. The cage itself also proved to be hazardous to the athletes: "Players would be thrown against the wire and most of us would get cut. The court would be covered with blood," said 5-foot-4 Barney Sedran, an early basketball star. Thanks to that chicken wire in Trenton, though, we now have the term "cager," another word for a basketball player.

## The First Baseball Game

On June 19, 1846, at the Elysian Fields in Hoboken, the very first baseball game was played. The game had been played in earlier forms, but this was the first time that modern rules applied, such as 90 feet between bases, a diamond-shaped field, formal lineups, and three outs per inning, to name a few. Two New York clubs—the Knickerbockers and the New York Nine—squared off against each other. The result? The New York Nine clobbered the Knickerbockers, 23–1, thus starting the tradition of New York teams playing in the Garden State.

# Hodgepodge, NJ

- Former president George W. Bush's Scottish terriers, Barney and Miss Beazley, were both born in New Jersey.

- Clarence Birdseye, the father of frozen food, first studied cooking as a student at Montclair High School.

- New Jersey has been home to the National Marbles Championship since 1960, when Wildwood first hosted the event where eight- to fourteen-year-olds compete in a game called Ringer.

- At 18, Rodney Dangerfield played his first gig as a comedian in Newark. He was paid only $2. Ten years later and tired of living hand-to-mouth, he took a hiatus from comedy, got married, settled down, and sold aluminum siding in Englewood.

- New Jersey has more nail salons per capita than any other U.S. state.

- Every summer, New Jerseyans consume more than a million ice-cream cones.

# Amazing Amber

*Leave the oil in Texas. California, keep your gold. We've got our own underground treasure.*

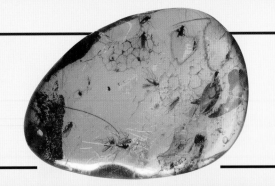

## Interesting Inclusions

Translucent and mysterious, amber has been valued as a precious gem since ancient times. Phoenicians roamed the seas to obtain it. The Romans considered it as valuable as gold. Folks in the Middle Ages sought its powers to fend off evil and black magic. Luckily for New Jerseyans, they've got an amber supply all their own in Sayreville in Middlesex County. But the jewelers have to fight off the

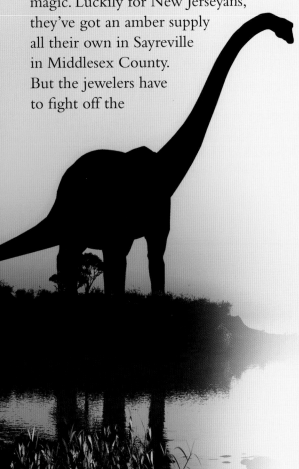

paleontologists to get their hands on these precious gems.

Because of how it forms, amber droplets can hold a wealth of information about the past. Amber starts out as a resin, the sticky stuff that a tree exudes to protect itself when it's injured or invaded by insects. When exposed to the air, tree resin usually dries out and crumbles. If the resin is protected from oxygen (like if it its buried under clay and silt), it will, over millions of years, fossilize into amber.

Before it hardens, though, the sticky resin sometimes traps bits from its environment. Feathers, animal hairs, plants, and insects become fossilized along with the resin. Called inclusions, these remnants of life on ancient earth, so fragile that they might not leave a fossil trace, are perfectly preserved inside bulbs of amber. Everything from flower pollen to the tiny hairs on insects can be seen just as it appeared millions of years ago.

## Science Goes Buggy

Amber was first found at the Sayreville Clay Mines during the 1800s. Large pits were dug to harvest the clay, and the workers also stumbled upon amber deposits. But it wasn't

*Resin oozes from a silver birch tree.*

until the early 1990s, when a fossil hunter dug into an abandoned pit and discovered amber that held an ancient insect, that interest in the area's amber really took off.

Age is what makes New Jersey's amber so special. Most amber found today, like that in the Baltic or the Dominican Republic, was formed 30 to 50 million years ago during the Tertiary period, after dinosaurs had become extinct. Only a few places on earth have amber from before that time—and one of those is Sayreville. So even though New Jersey doesn't have the largest deposits of amber in the United States, it has the only substantial North American deposits that date back to the Cretaceous period—65 to 135 million years ago.

During the Cretaceous period, dinosaurs were still around, and flowering plants and modern insects began to emerge. Sayreville's amber and its inclusions contain perfectly preserved specimens of life from that time. David Grimaldi, curator and chairman of entomology at the American Museum of Natural History in New York

1 mm

*This wasp fossil was preserved in amber more than 60 million years ago.*

*Right and below: Sayerville Clay Mines. Workers inadvertently found amber while mining the area for clay.*

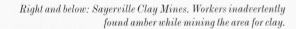

City, has found New Jersey amber with inclusions that date back as far as 95 million years. He and other paleontologists have discovered more than 100 species of insects and plants trapped inside the petrified resin. In fact, Sayreville's amber has housed the world's oldest…

- Ant—the first proof that ants lived during the age of dinosaurs.

- Mosquito—with a mouth tough enough to bite a dinosaur!

- Mushroom—*Archaeomarasmius leggetti*. It's 90 to 94 million years old.

- Bee—*Trigona prisca*, which flew for the last time about 65 to 80 million years ago.

# NJ on TV

*You might spot some familiar buildings and landscapes when you're flipping channels—several TV shows are set in the Garden State. Here are some of the Jersey-based series on our watch list.*

## "Family" Man

*The Sopranos* (1999–2007) is quintessentially New Jersey—from its opening title sequence to the suburban neighborhood of mob boss Tony Soprano (James Gandolfini) to his gang's gathering spots and watering holes. For the opening credits, a film crew drove around North Jersey with a handheld camcorder, capturing scenes of everyday life: the Lincoln Tunnel, the Jersey Turnpike, a cemetery, a meat market. The exterior shots of the Soprano home were filmed at an actual residence in North Caldwell. When Tony's mom Livia moves into a seniors' home, that's Green Hill Retirement Home in West Orange. Indoor and outdoor scenes of the Bada Bing gentlemen's club, one of Tony Soprano's hangouts, took place at Lodi's Satin Dolls (whose real-life owner had Mafia ties and was convicted of racketeering and extortion in 2013). Even a *Sopranos* episode set in Maine was shot in Jersey—when Tony and his daughter, Meadow, tour colleges in Maine, they actually filmed at Drew University in Madison, and their motel was in Bergen County. Other real

locations in the show are Holsten's ice cream parlor in Bloomfield, the Cleveland Auto Body Shop in Harrison, and Skyway Diner in Kearny, though the last two have closed.

*Left: Some of* The Sopranos *cast*
*Above: Holstein's in Bloomfield*

## Wellesville, NJ?

One TV show with surprisingly enduring popularity is *The Adventures of Pete & Pete,* which debuted on Nickelodeon in 1993. It followed the lives of two redhead brothers (Mike Maronna and Danny Tamberelli) who were kind of weird and also, strangely, both named Pete. Set in a fictional town called Wellesville, the series was obviously filmed in New Jersey (though the state is never mentioned in the show). The Petes live in a neighborhood with tree-lined streets—it was filmed in South Orange and Leonia. Their school scenes took place in Bayonne, Cranford, and Nutley. Sharp-eyed viewers also catch glimpses of New Jersey Transit buses, the Kill Van Kull channel in Bayonne, and the Willowbrook Mall in Wayne. The series ran for only three seasons, but more than two decades later, its special reunion events still sell out. According to the show's creators, Chris Viscardi and William McRobb, die-hard fans love that the kids on the show "were off the beaten path a little bit." McRobb says fans often mention how important the show was when the fans were growing up, and say, "Thank God somebody was making a show about me, because no other shows were about me."

## Monopoly City

Since its premiere in 2010, the mob drama *Boardwalk Empire* has drawn such wide appeal that it was even one of President Barack Obama's favorite series. The main character Nucky (Steve Buscemi) is based on Enoch "Nucky" Johnson, the politician and crime kingpin who ran Atlantic City during Prohibition. Several locations that the real Nucky frequented appear in the show and are still open today, including the 1880 James' Salt Water Taffy store and factory; its competitor Fralinger's, also from the 1880s; the Knife & Fork Inn, a men's-only pub and steakhouse; and the Ritz-Carlton Hotel, which is now the Ritz Condominiums. However, the locations you see in the show are re-creations built for the *Boardwalk Empire* set in Brooklyn, not the actual Atlantic City locations. (Fooled ya!)

*The Knife & Fork Inn*

## His Cakes Take the Cake

The reality show *Cake Boss* centers on Carlo's Bake Shop, a family-run bakery in Hoboken. Buddy "Cake Boss" Valastro is a fourth-generation baker who works with much of his family—including four sisters, two brothers-in-law, and a cousin—to create elaborate concoctions for special events. In one episode, the staff of Adventure Aquarium in Camden throws a going-away party for the famed 14-foot alligator named Mighty Mike, who's being transferred to a different facility. So Valastro baked a giant cake replica of the gator with remote-controlled jaws that opened and closed. For the Coney Island Side Show, the team made a topsy-turvy stacked cake with freak show scenes, sideshow banners, and curtains. The shop has become so famous that its street has been renamed Carlo's Bakery Way, and new shops are opening across the state in Morristown, Red Bank, Ridgewood, Westfield, and Marlton.

## Dr. Detective

In the Emmy-winning series *House* (2004–12), Hugh Laurie plays Dr. Gregory House, who's like the Sherlock Holmes of the medical world. Using his intuition, lie-detection skills, and medical expertise, he diagnoses patients who have mysterious ailments. The show is set at the Princeton–Plainsboro Teaching Hospital, a fictional hospital at Princeton University. Aerial shots of the building might look familiar, though—that's Frist Campus Center at Princeton. For the scenes at Mayfield Psychiatric Hospital, the *House* crew visited the Greystone Park Psychiatric Hospital in Parsippany. Built in 1876, the imposing stone-and-brick building looks just as creepy as you'd expect, considering that it's an abandoned, 500,000-square-foot former insane asylum where doctors used to perform lobotomies and shock therapy.

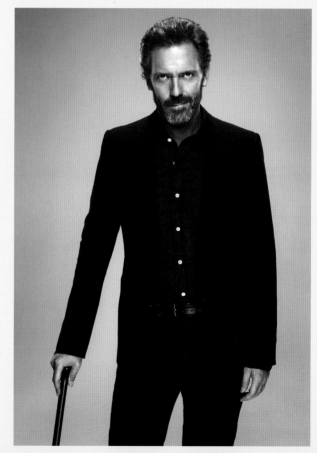

*Actor Hugh Laurie portrayed Dr. House.*

# Ivy League Antics, Part II

*On page 18, we introduced some of Princeton University's wackier traditions. Didn't have enough? Here are three more.*

*Hodder Hall (above and left) was a main site of Princeton's Nude Olpympics.*

## Nude Olympics

Nothing says "smart" like a sophomore running through the snow with only a hat, boots, and a smile. Nobody knows exactly how or why the Nude Olympics began, but sometime in the 1970s, it became tradition for sophomores to run naked through one of the campus courtyards on the evening of the year's first snowfall. At first, the streaking actually involved events—wheelbarrow and three-legged races—but it quickly degenerated into running laps and campuswide antics. In 1976 overenthusiastic Nude Olympians even ran into the university's pool, where they interrupted a swim meet. Over the next 20 years, the event became an established ritual, anticipated by sophomores as a rite of passage.

Alas, a tradition like this couldn't go on forever, and in 1999 its time was up. During the 1997-98 school year, not a single flake of snow fell on the Princeton campus, so the sophomore class missed out on the event. The following year, when snow came on January 8, 1999, the campus was in for some trouble. The current crop of sophomores had never seen how the event should go; meanwhile the packs of juniors who felt cheated out of their own Olympics joined these games, and things quickly got out of hand. Six students were hospitalized for overconsumption of alcohol, property was damaged, the press was all over it, and the university was embarrassed. So the administration banned the event, threatening any student who participated in something even remotely similar to the Nude Olympics with a year's suspension.

116

## Fountain of Knowledge

In front of the Woodrow Wilson School of Public Policy, called "Woody Woo" by the students who major in it, is a reflecting pool with a pinnacled sculpture called the Fountain of Freedom in the center. Officially, there is no swimming allowed in the fountain, but unofficially, graduating Woody Woo seniors can take a dip on the day that they turn in their theses in early April. They gather at 5:00 p.m. to hand in their papers, don a commemorative T-shirt, and dash into the fountain.

After each home football game that Princeton wins, the Princeton University Band also marches through the fountain in celebration. The university seems to have resigned itself to this tradition as well: a renovation of the reflecting pool even added steps descending invitingly into the water.

## It's Not the Grades, It's the Gates

Since 1970, as the final act of graduation, Princeton students walk out through the school's main gates—called the FitzRandolph Gates—and into the "real world." Before 1970 the gates remained closed except for a few special occasions, such as the university's bicentennial. When the gates were permanently opened that year, a superstition spontaneously emerged: If you walk out of those gates as a student, you will never graduate. Some students ignore the story, but most go out of their way to avoid the gates. Why risk it?

*Top and above: Students and the Princeton University B and take a dip in the Woody Woo reflecting pool.*

*The FitzRandolph Gates*

# Cruise to Catastrophe

*The last sailing of the* Morro Castle *was a mysterious voyage to disaster.*

*Crowds gather to watch the damaged* Morro Castle *return to port in 1934.*

## Trouble in Paradise

On September 8, 1934, crowds flocked to the boardwalk in Asbury Park and strained to see the smoldering remains of the SS *Morro Castle*. The once-elegant luxury liner now lay shipwrecked near the convention center. The captain had died mysteriously during the ship's final voyage from Cuba to New York. And only a few hours after his death, a terrible fire had raged through the ship, costing the lives of 134 people. However, few in the crowd knew that the luxury liner had problems long before it caught fire and foundered off the shores of New Jersey. Over the next 70 years, the shipwreck would remain a controversial mystery, complete with tales of scandal and rumors of murder.

The *Morro Castle*, named for a 16th-century fortress on Cuba's Havana Bay, was a four-year-old, 11,520-ton steamship liner operated by the Ward Line. Known for its fine food, entertainment, and modern accommodations, the *Morro Castle* took wealthy tourists from New York to Havana, Cuba, and back. Carrying 316 passengers and 230 officers and crew, it was considered a state-of-the-art vessel and one of the safest ships at sea. But the glitzy *Morro* had a darker side.

## "Awful Slop"

While the passengers sailed in the lap of luxury, the crew didn't have such a cushy arrangement. During the Great Depression, workers were desperate for jobs, and the Ward Line needed to save money. Many of the crew lacked training, and rumors abounded that many of their

*Top: The* Morro Castle *burns at sea.*
*Bottom: Passengers escape the burning ship in a lifeboat.*

seaman's papers had been forged. The crew complained of long working hours, low pay, and extremely poor working conditions. One sailor reported that the officers and passengers ate gourmet, while the crew existed on "awful slop."

Captain Robert R. Wilmott, who commanded the *Morro Castle*, often butted heads with junior officers and crew, especially since some crew members subsidized their low wages with a bit of smuggling on the side. They smuggled just about everything—from narcotics and Cuban rum to illegal immigrants and political asylum seekers.

Contraband hidden on the ship was ferried from Havana into New York, and Captain Wilmott constantly had to break up these minismuggling rings. According to some historians, the tension between the captain and his crew reached a dangerous pitch by the time the *Morro Castle* set out on its last voyage to New York.

## A Brewing Storm

On September 7, when the ship was about six miles away from New Jersey, a storm blew up in the Atlantic Ocean and buffeted the ship with gale-force winds. But Captain Wilmott wasn't at the helm. In fact Wilmott, who usually dined with the passengers, stayed in his quarters suffering from stomach pain. Later that night, the ship's doctor declared that Wilmott had died of a heart attack in his stateroom. Without its captain, the ship continued to sail. Meanwhile, passengers—who thought they'd soon be docking in New York—danced at the traditional farewell ball.

After Wilmott's death, command of the ship passed to First Officer William Warms, who accepted the new title while he contended with the raging storm that continued through the night. To add to the new captain's problems, at 2:15 a.m. a passenger saw smoke coming out of a locker near the writing room on the promenade deck. The locker was on fire. The crew rushed to extinguish the flames, but failed; fire spread once the locker doors were opened and the storm's heavy winds fanned it. Within an hour, the blaze was out of control.

*A fireboat douses the* Morro Castle's *flames.*

*Radioman George Rogers was hailed a hero after the* Morro Castle *fire... but was he really?*

## Ship of Shame

Acting Captain Warms tried to get his ship to safety but failed to order an SOS for help, so radioman George Rogers, acting on his own initiative, did it. He battled heat and smoke to send out the first distress call at about 3:24 a.m. and was later hailed as a hero. There were other heroes among the crew, who worked to save lives and who stuck to their posts. But their courage was overshadowed by the accounts of angry passengers who survived.

Some of the underpaid and poorly trained crew apparently didn't hang around during the disaster. Warms, still trying to steer the ship to safety, had given no order to abandon ship, but crew members commandeered the lifeboats and rowed for the Jersey Shore, eight miles away. Chief Engineer Eban Abbot was said to have ordered his crew to stay at their posts belowdecks—while he leapt into a lifeboat. Of the first 98 survivors to reach the shore, only six were passengers.

Most of the passengers—who'd never gone through a fire drill or a lifeboat drill on the *Morro Castle*—had to fend for themselves. Supplied with life preservers, many jumped into the deathly cold waters of the Atlantic. Some swam toward the shore; others tried to stay afloat until rescue ships arrived. For the older and weaker passengers, rescue didn't come soon enough. More than 100 of the 134 people who died that night were passengers who either burned to death or drowned.

## Castle Controversy

When the smoke cleared, the investigation concluded that an "act of God" had destroyed the luxury liner. Investigators noted that highly flammable blankets were stored in the locker where the fire broke out. The blankets rested against a wall facing a smokestack, which could have overheated and started the fire. But rumors of crime persisted.

The rumors claimed that Captain Wilmott had actually been poisoned by one of the crew members running the smuggling ring who would have been fired—or even prosecuted—when the voyage was over. Then arson was committed to hide the murder.

*A rescue crew pulls survivors to safety.*

## A Flaming Murderer?

That theory gained credibility when the heroic radioman George Rogers later proved himself a deadly criminal. After the shipwreck, Rogers opened a radio repair shop, but the shop burned down in a fire as mysterious as the one on the ship. Rogers then joined the Bayonne police force, but was convicted of attempted murder when he mailed a bomb to his supervisor. After emerging from prison in the 1950s, Rogers was sent back for life for murdering two of his neighbors. Rogers also had a juvenile criminal record involving fire, and he was labeled by some authorities as a pyromaniac.

Did Rogers commit both murder and arson on the luxury liner? One crew member later recalled that Captain Wilmott disliked and distrusted Rogers, calling him a "bad man." Rogers might have been worried about being dismissed in disgrace, but after the disaster struck, the fire brought him medals and fame. Thomas Gallagher, author of the history *Fire at Sea*, visited Rogers in prison to ask the convict if he had started the *Morro Castle* fire, but Rogers refused to answer.

More than 80 years after the tragedy, no version of what happened that night can prove that murder or arson occurred.

More controversy surrounded the rapid spread of the fire, the failure to send out a timely distress call, and the lack of help getting the passengers into lifeboats. Acting Captain Warms was tried, convicted, and sentenced to two years in prison for negligence. But he claimed he did his best, and the ruling was later overturned. Chief Engineer Abbot got four years, with his sentence overturned, too. To escape bad publicity, the Ward Line changed its name and continued doing business as the Cuba Mail Line until 1959.

## Not in Vain

Despite all the unsolved mysteries, one fact is clear: the *Morro Castle* fire had an impact on cruise ship safety. After that terrible shipwreck, the United States government took notice and became convinced that more federal involvement in maritime training was necessary. Congressional hearings led to the Merchant Marine Act of 1936, which mandadted tougher safety regulations, including lifeboat drills for passengers. The *Morro Castle* disaster also led to the creation of the U.S. Merchant Marine Academy, where seafaring men and women can be educated and trained for their profession.

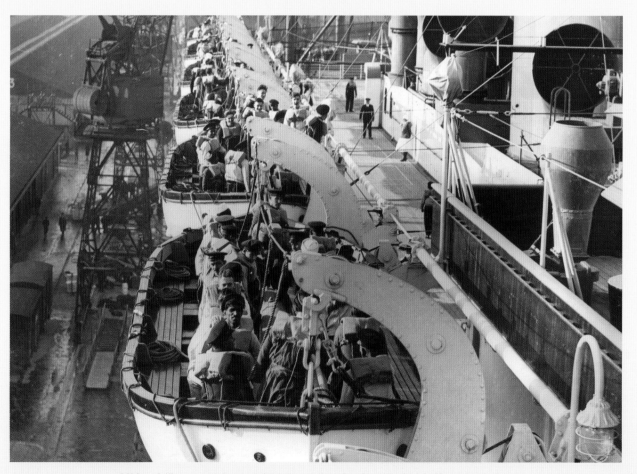

*Lifeboat drills were one of many safety measures introduced as a result of the* Morro Castle *disaster.*

# What Exit?

*According to a popular joke, New Jerseyans identify where they live not by their towns' names but by their exit numbers on the Garden State Parkway. But the Parkway is so much more than that.*

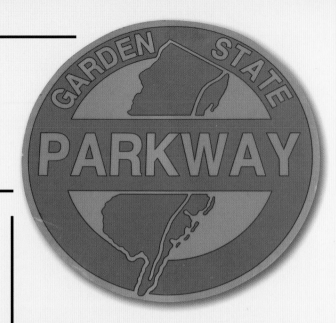

*Traffic backs up on the Parkway.*

## All Points South

The Garden State Parkway (called just the Parkway by locals) may have gotten a bad rap. Like its sister highway, the New Jersey Turnpike, the Parkway was designed with the most modern highway innovations in mind in order to be the smoothest ride in the state. When it opened, it was called the Parkway with a Heart, and it was supposed to make life easier.

After World War II, New Jersey's roads were clogged with cars trying to get from New York City to the resorts down the shore. The state legislature decided in 1945 to build a superhighway to ease some of the congestion. They were planning to pay for it in tax dollars, but over the next five years, they managed to build only 18 miles of road. And those miles weren't even connected. Something had to be done to speed things up and bring in more funds for the project.

The brilliant solution the legislators devised was tolls. Using the New Jersey Turnpike as an example, the legistlature decided to issue bonds to pay for the construction. Payments on interest and the principal would then be covered by the tolls. With the new plan of a self-sustaining toll road, they were able to finance the construction with more than $300 million of government bonds. In less than three years, the Garden State Parkway was ready for business.

## Vital Stats

The Parkway officially opened on July 1, 1955, when Governor Robert Meyner paid the first toll at the Paramus toll plaza. The Parkway's first chief engineer, Harold Giffin—inventor of the traffic circle, the cloverleaf, and the reflecting curb—featured his innovation, the "singing shoulder," on the Parkway (they're better known as rumble strips, the grooves on the shoulder that rattle your car when you drift out of your lane). The road was built for safety, comfort, and speed—an important feature for tourists who couldn't wait to get to the beach.

The Parkway now stretches from Cape May, up the shore 173 miles to the New York border, where it connects with the New York Thruway. Along its most congested stretch, the Garden State Parkway hosts 200,000 vehicles a day. When it was built, the Parkway had

Toll Plaza on the Garden State Parkway of New Jersey. 88409 13

Birdseye View Asbury Toll Plaza and the Garden State Parkway of 88407 11 New Jersey.

Aerial View of the Garden State Parkway, looking South in Monmouth 88408 12 County towards Red Bank, N.J.

*Vintage postcards show the Parkway as it was imagined: wide lanes and no congestion.*

four lanes in most places. But as traffic congestion worsened, the government added a lane by building onto the shoulder and shaving a foot or so off existing lanes. This makes driving the Parkway a white-knuckle experience for most out-of-staters.

The roadway curves gradually back and forth along its entire length, whether it has to or not. This design is to prevent drivers from being lulled to sleep by the monotony of a straight road.

## Taking Its Toll

- Unlike most toll roads where you pay at the on-ramp or exit ramp, there are tollbooths plopped in the middle of the road on the Parkway. Some are just six miles apart. These barrier tolls cause long traffic jams, especially during rush hour. Why would anyone design a road with

inherent traffic jams? For the drivers' benefit, of course. According to the designers of the road, "One criticism of today's expressways is the tedium and hypertension they create within the driver. A short 'break' en route… relieves the monotony."

- Until 2011, the Garden State Parkway toll plazas operated on the honor system: Drivers who didn't have enough money when they passed through could pick up an envelope and mail the toll in later. Only 4 percent of those envelopes were ever returned, though, costing the state more than $100,000 a year in lost tolls. Now, if you drive through without paying, cameras snap a photo of your license plate and you'll get a bill for the toll…and a $50 fee.

*Traffic backs up at a toll booth.*

# More Jersey Speak

### Pineys
When Jerseyans mention a Piney, they're not talking about trees. Pineys are people who live in the Pinelands.

### Route
When giving directions, Jerseyans put the word route (pronounced like "root") in front of the highway number. It's not "the 46," it's "Route 46."

### Self-service Gas Stations
You'll never hear this term because these don't exist in New Jersey.

### Shoobie
A derogatory term locals use for tourists at the Jersey Shore. There are two stories behind its origins. The first: shoobies are people who wear their shoes at the beach. The other: day-trippers once brought their lunches to the beach in shoeboxes.

*Shoobies pack the Jersey Shore.*

123

# Hometowns: Cape May

*Located at the southernmost tip of the state, Cape May's beaches and Victorian buildings have made it a great place to get away from it all for centuries now.*

## The Stats

**Location:** Cape May County

**Founding:** That's a little tricky. Cape May County was officially chartered in 1692, but settlers had been living there since the 1630s. The resort of Cape May, a separate city within the county, became popular in the early 19th century and was officially incorporated in 1869.

**Current Population:** 3,570

**Size:** 2.3 square miles

*Above: Tourists hit the beach at Cape May.*

## What's in a Name?

Cape May County was named after Cornelius Jacobsen Mey, the Dutch captain who first explored the territory in the 1620s. So it's not clear if the city is technically named after the county, the explorer, or both.

*Above and below: Cape May's unique architecture*

## Claims to Fame

- Cape May remains the oldest seashore resort in the United States.

*President Ulysses S. Grant*

- Presidents Franklin Pierce, James Buchanan, Ulysses S. Grant, and Benjamin Harrison all vacationed here.

- A beachcomber's delight, Cape May "diamonds" are milky quartz pebbles that wash up on the beaches. When polished, they can be cut like gemstones. Most of the stones are pebble-sized, but a Cape May diamond that weighed more than three pounds was discovered in the 19th century.

- Every Labor Day weekend, the International Clamshell Pitching Club of Cape May holds its annual tournament, where competitors try to toss shells into 5½-inch-wide holes that are 25½ feet apart on hard-packed sand.

- For more than three decades, the New Jersey Audubon Society has hosted the World Series of Birdwatching in Cape May. This annual ornithological competition is always held on the second Saturday in May. Thousands of avid birders fly in from around the world to compete and determine which team can find and identify, by sound or sight, the most varieties of wildfowl in a 24-hour period. The current record is 270 sightings in the daylong search.

*Cape May birds, clockwise from top: the mute swan, osprey, and warbler*

*Above: Cape May "diamonds" like these are prized by beachcombers.*

*Right: Participants keep watch during the 2010 World Series of Birdwatching.*

# My Bedroom for a Horse!

*One of America's first liberated women came from New Jersey, and her patriotic duty was inspired by her love for her horse.*

*General "Mad" Anthony Wayne*

## "Mad" Man's Mutiny

Temperance Wick, known as Tempe (rhymes with Shempy), was the youngest of five children of Captain Henry Wick, who owned a farm near Morristown's Jockey Hollow, the site of the 1779–80 winter encampment for George Washington's Continental Army. A wealthy farmer and cavalryman, Captain Wick owned 1,400 acres of woods and fields that he gladly let the army use as needed during the Revolutionary War. Visiting officers would often stay with the Wick family in their large, wood-frame home.

The most popular version of Tempe's story begins in January 1781, when the Morristown area around the Wick farm was home to the soldiers of the Pennsylvania Line under the command of General "Mad" Anthony Wayne. The men had endured freezing weather, inadequate food, and no wages for more than a year. But they became infuriated when news arrived that new recruits were getting a handsome bounty to sign on while they shivered and starved with no money to show for it. So the soldiers decided to mutiny on New Year's Day. They abandoned their Morristown posts and vowed to return to Pennsylvania to take up their cause.

## Horsey Heroine

Meanwhile, Tempe (born in 1751) was an accomplished rider and thoroughly familiar with the local countryside. One January morning she was sent out on her large, white steed to fetch medicine for her ailing mother. On the way home, six of the

*Revolutionary War reenactors abandon their posts at Morristown and begin the mutiny.*

A mural at the Morristown National Historic Park shows the layout of Washington's army's encampment at Wick Farm in 1779–80. The soldiers' camp (far right) sat very close to the family's farm (left).

mutinous Pennsylvania soldiers stopped her and demanded that she give them her horse. She had no intention of letting them steal it, though, so while pretending to dismount, she instead slapped the reins and took off, leaving the startled men behind. One fired a shot in her direction, but Tempe and her horse were soon out of sight.

With the soldiers in pursuit, Tempe knew that it would be just a matter of time before they arrived at her farm. If she took her beloved steed to the barn, they would surely find and take him. So the quick-thinking Tempe brought the horse to the back door and coaxed him into the house, through the kitchen and into the guest bedroom. She closed the one small window in the room, plunging it into darkness, and muffled the sound of the horse's hooves with her feather bedding. There, the pair waited.

*Morristown National Historic Park includes re-creations of the log cabins used by George Washington's soldiers during the winter of 1779–80.*

## Pay No Attention to That Horse Behind the Curtain

When the mutinous soldiers arrived at the farm, they thoroughly searched the barn and pastures. No horse. They waited for Tempe and the horse to return, never thinking to look in the house. Eventually they gave up and moved on. How long Tempe and the horse remained inside cannot be verified—some say three days, others say three weeks. Hoof marks were supposedly visible in the house for quite some time after the war ended. News of Tempe Wick's courageous

act spread throughout the colonies, and she is remembered as one of the first Revolutionary War heroines.

Tempe married Captain William Tuttle a few years later, had five children, and lived until 1822. She is buried at the Evergreen Cemetery in Morristown. The Wick house was restored to its original condition in 1934 and can be visited today as part of the Morristown National Historical Park.

*Inside a courthouse in Flemington, the jury was selected while a grieving father and an accused murderer sat close enough to touch each other. The story of the Lindbergh baby's kidnapping (which began on page 98) continues.*

*Above: Hauptmann's arrest made the front page of many newspapers.*

*Right: Reporters and onlookers swarm the Hauptmann house.*

## Making a Case

The trial began on January 2, 1935, and it was a media circus. Celebrities such as comedian Jack Benny, novelist Damon Runyon, and influential journalist Walter Winchell were among the 60,000 spectators. State troopers had to form a human chain to protect the courthouse. Street vendors even hawked souvenirs—everything from forged autographs of Charles Lindbergh Sr. to phony locks of hair supposedly from little Charlie's head.

New Jersey's attorney general, David T. Wilentz, acted as the prosecutor, and he asserted that greed was the motive for the crime; Hauptmann had lost a significant amount of money in the stock market and kidnapped the baby for the sizable ransom the wealthy Lindberghs could pay. He used a homemade ladder to break into the Lindbergh home, took the baby, and left behind a ransom demand. Wilentz asserted that Hauptmann killed little Charlie in his crib so he wouldn't cry out, though he also suggested the baby could have died from a fall when the ladder broke as the kidnapper fled. After the baby's death, Hauptmann buried the body in nearby woods on the side of the road.

The dramatic defense attorney, Edward "Big Ed" Reilly, was hired by the Hearst newspapers, ensuring that the media circus wasn't squashed, and he offered a different version of events: Hauptmann was home with his wife, Anna, on March 1, 1932.

*Above: Trial evidence included various items from Hauptmann's garage.*

The kidnapping was actually a conspiracy between Hauptmann's shadowy business partner, furrier Isidor Fisch, and someone on Lindbergh's staff.

## Witness for the Prosecution

The prosecution's case was strong, and it rested on a few things:

- **Hauptmann's Criminal Record:** In Germany, Hauptmann had served time for burglary. In one of his crimes, he had used a ladder.

- **Clues in Hauptmann's Garage:** The Lindbergh bills were found there. The ladder used in the kidnapping was partly constructed from a beam in the garage attic. Jafsie Condon's phone number was also written inside a closet.

- **Ransom Notes:** Handwriting experts testified that samples of Hauptmann's writing matched the writing on ransom notes—including one in the nursery. Hauptmann's private papers also revealed some of the same grammar mistakes and misspelled words that the kidnapper used.

*An FBI agent fingerprints Bruno Hauptmann.*

- **Witnesses:** A taxi driver and Condon had both seen Cemetery John. Lindbergh had heard his voice. All three testified that Hauptmann was Cemetery John.

- **Money:** At the same time that Cemetery John picked up his money, Hauptmann quit working as a carpenter and started living off "stock investments."

## Sowing Reasonable Doubt

The defense argued that Hauptmann was the wrong man for the following reasons:

- **Planted Evidence:** The defense claimed that the police had written Jafsie Condon's phone number on the garage wall and stolen the board from Hauptmann's garage to claim it was part of the kidnapper's ladder.

  - **Police Intimidation:** Hauptmann was roughed up by police and forced to imitate the handwriting on the ransom notes for the prosecution's handwriting experts.

  - **It Was an Inside Job:** Hauptmann wouldn't know how to pick out the nursery window at Hopewell, a huge house with 20 rooms. And he couldn't know that the Lindbergh baby would be at Hopewell, since the family usually spent weekdays in Englewood. Plus, the Lindberghs'

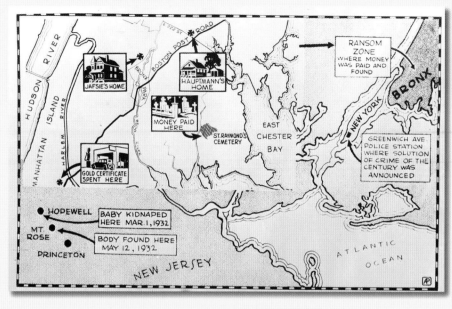

*A map shows the Lindbergh kidnapping crime scene.*

dog never barked—as it surely would have if a stranger were on the grounds.

- **The Kidnapper Was Fisch:** Isidor Fisch, a German immigrant, became Hauptmann's friend and business partner in 1932. The pair agreed to equally split the profits of Hauptmann's stock investments and Fisch's fur business. According to the defense, Fisch left for Germany in 1933 and gave Hauptmann "papers" in a shoe box for safekeeping. Hauptmann discovered that the box was actually full of (the ransom) money. Since Fisch owed him money, Hauptmann kept and spent it. The defense claimed Fisch conspired with Violet Sharpe and other members of the Lindberghs' staff to kidnap the baby. Fisch died in Germany in 1934, so he couldn't answer to the accusation.

- **Hauptmann's Alibi:** Anna Hauptmann testified that she'd been with her husband on the night of the kidnapping.

*Above: Hauptmann was tried in this courtroom at the Hunterdon County Courthouse.*

*Left: Defense attorney Edward Reilly (left) consults with his client.*

## A Rush to Judgment?

Historians agree that the Lindbergh trial went better for the prosecution than for the defense. Some on the jury took Reilly's theatrics for arrogance. The defense brought in witnesses who had credibility problems. And a decision to have Hauptmann testify backfired when he failed to convince jurors that there were reasonable explanations for the ransom money found in his garage. (Reporters and Wilentz called Hauptmann's explanation a "Fisch story.") Plus, Hauptmann's testimony allowed the prosecution to admit evidence of his character, including his crimes in Germany.

In the end, the jury took 11 hours to declare Hauptmann guilty. The prisoner was taken to the New Jersey State Prison in Trenton, where he was executed in the electric chair on April 3, 1936.

## Is the Jury Still Out?

Though the prosecution and defense have long since rested their cases, history never did. Hauptmann never confessed, even though he was told it was his best chance to avoid the death penalty. A newspaper promised to give Hauptmann's family $75,000 in return for details of the kidnapping. Yet Hauptmann still insisted on his innocence. The Lindbergh family, however, believed that justice was served.

Months before Hauptmann's execution, Lindbergh and his family left the country to live in seclusion in England. Meanwhile, Anna Hauptmann campaigned tirelessly to clear her husband's name. Many began to believe her. Books and movies appeared

*Anna Hauptmann (left) always insisted on her husband's innocence.*

arguing that police had manufactured evidence against Hauptmann and that the baby was killed either by someone on the staff or even in the family. One revisionist theory claims Lindbergh himself accidentally killed the baby. To this day, authors, historians, and crime buffs continue to debate the trial's verdict.

## The Scene of the Crime

The Lindberghs deserted their Hopewell estate, donating it to New Jersey. Today their airstrip is woodland again. The estate, including the house, is now the Albert Elias Residential Group Center, a residential home for juveniles. Visitors still occasionally arrive to see the window that once looked in on the Lindbergh nursery.

*Above: Charles Lindbergh testifies at Bruno Hauptmann's trial.*
*Below: The New Jersey State Prison in Trenton*

*Charles Lindbergh (center) and H. Norman Schwarzkopf (right) leave the courthouse during Hauptmann's trial.*

# Jersey Originals

*These local characters give their state extra depth, color, and charm.*

*Passaic Falls, where Sam Patch made a giant leap in 1827*

*Floyd Vivino in 2009*

## The Jersey Jumper

Sam Patch first gained fame in 1827 when he took a flying leap off 77-foot-high Passaic Falls in Paterson. Patch's newfound celebrity convinced him to quit his day job at a cotton mill to devote himself full time to his career as the Jersey Jumper. Patch took his act on the road and jumped off of high places all over the country. In 1829 he became the first person to go over Niagara Falls—without a barrel—and survive. Patch's daring eventually caught up with him later that year, when he died attempting to dive over Genesee Falls in Rochester, New York.

## A New Jersey Jersey Cow

A Jersey cow named You'll Do Lobelia was christened Borden's first official Elsie in 1939 at the New York World's Fair. The newly dubbed Elsie went on to become one of the world's most famous mascots; she appeared in movies and even toured cross-country in her car, the Cowdillac. Sadly, after being seriously injured in a traffic accident in 1941, the first Elsie returned to her home at the Gordon-Walker Farm in Plainsboro, where she was put to sleep and buried under a headstone that reads "A Pure Bred Jersey Cow. One of the Great Elsies of Our Time."

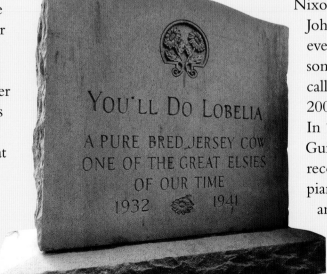

*The headstone for Elsie the cow*

## Who's Your Uncle?

Floyd Vivino, a Paterson-born Jersey native, is a multitalented man: singer, piano player, puppeteer, and actor, but he was best known as the porkpie hat–wearing host of the *Uncle Floyd Show,* New Jersey's longest-running television program. It ran from 1974 to 1998 and was a low-budget collection of skits, gags, puppet cohosts, and musical guests—including the Ramones, Jon Bon Jovi, and Cyndi Lauper. This variety show had lots of fans, including Richard Nixon, David Bowie, and John Lennon. Bowie even recorded a tribute song to Uncle Floyd called "Slip Away, on his 2002 album *Heathen.* In 1999 Vivino set a Guinness-verified world record for nonstop piano playing—24 hours and 25 minutes.

132

# Are You There, Judy?

*Nearly anything you need to know about the "Awkward Years," aka puberty, can be explained via the books of Judy Blume.*

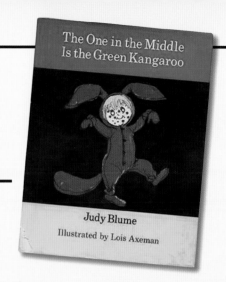

## Becoming a Desperate Housewife

Judy Blume was born Judy Sussman in Elizabeth, New Jersey, in 1938, and could easily have been one of the characters she wrote about in her books. She said in 2004: "I was a small, shy, anxious child with eczema, as fearful as Sheila the Great, as imaginative as Sally J. Freedman." As a girl, she was also an avid reader—but not of children's books. The reason: "I never found my kind of reality in children's books. No child was anything like me. No child thought the kinds of things I did, leading me to believe I definitely wasn't normal."

The young Ms. Sussman was determined to lead a "normal" life, however. She became Judy Blume in 1959 by getting married (while still in college), and she was a mother by 1961. But by the mid-1960s, the 20-something housewife was going nuts out in the suburbs. "I adored my children, but inside was an empty space, a gnawing, an ache that I couldn't identify, one that I didn't understand," she said. To fill that empty space, Blume went back to her childhood, resurrected her imagination, and began to write.

Her career didn't start auspiciously, however, as the rejections piled up. One of Blume's earliest rejections was from *Highlights* magazine. The home of such immortal fare as "Goofus and Gallant"

*Judy Blume in 1981*

informed Blume that her work did "not win in competition with others." After that particular rejection, Blume hid in a closet and cried. It was two years before she sold her first book, *The One in the Middle Is the Green Kangaroo*, in 1969.

## Cornering the Market

But it was Blume's third book that began her transformation into America's Muse of Puberty. *Are You There God? It's Me,*

*Margaret*, published in 1970, featured a girl dealing with both her confusion over religion (she was the child of an interfaith marriage) and her anxiety over being one of puberty's "late bloomers." Neither subject had been directly tackled in adolescent fiction, and to hit both at the same time made a definite impression.

Throughout her career, Blume kept talking about difficult subjects. She wrote books that touched on bullying, divorce, losing one's virginity, and the overall awkwardness of existence when you're in the space between pigtails and cocktails. And because she wrote in voice that kids could relate to, Judy Blume became one of the most popular kids' authors of all time.

*Judy Blume's first literary hit*

133

## She Writes Banned Books

Naturally, all that frank discussion of touchy subjects eventually ran afoul of some adults. One night, Blume received a phone call from a woman who asked if she were the author of *Margaret*. When she said yes, the woman called her a communist and slammed down the phone. "I never did figure out if she equated communism with menstruation or religion," wrote Blume. The principal of her children's elementary school refused to put *Margaret* in the library because he felt the topic was inappropriate, despite the high probability that some of his sixth-grade female students had already personally dealt with the subjects at hand.

By the early 1980s, Blume's books increasingly became a target for organized censors, who complained that the novels were inappropriate for children because of language and subject matter. *Margaret* and *Then Again, Maybe I Won't* (which covered puberty for boys) weren't the only targets: even Blume's 1974 book *Blubber*, which featured a girl being mercilessly teased by her classmates, was protested because it didn't show the girl's tormentors being punished. Blume's response was that in real life, sometimes tormentors aren't punished—which was a lesson in itself. As a result of the push to get her books removed from school libraries, Blume often found herself near the top of the list of America's most banned authors.

## Winning Is the Best Revenge

Despite the best efforts of the censors, Blume's 22 books (including three for adult readers) have sold more than 65 million copies combined. Blume's influence on entire generations of teens and preteens—and her fight against censorship—was enough for the National Book Foundation to present her with an honorary National Book Award in 2004, elevating her into the highest ranks of American letters with previous recipients such as Eudora Welty, Toni Morrison, John Updike, and Philip Roth. For those still not convinced of Blume's importance, a 1998 article in the *Boston Phoenix* weekly put it best: "Presumably, puberty would have happened without Judy Blume books, but there's no way to know for sure."

*Judy Blume's books have sold more than 65 million copies.*

# Fake Newsman Extraordinaire!

*Jon Stewart accepts his Emmy Award in 2011.*

- Jon Stuart (Leibowitz) was born on November 28, 1962, in Trenton.

- He graduated from the College of William and Mary in Williamsburg, Virginia. ("I wanted to explore the rich tapestry of Judaica that is Southern Virginia.") In college Stewart was a member of the men's soccer team. An award in his honor, the Leibo, is given out annually to the team member who makes his teammates laugh the most in a season.

- Before turning to stand-up, Stewart had an array of interesting jobs: He was a Woolworth's stockboy in Quaker Bridge Mall, where he destroyed $10,000 worth of tropical fish aquariums and was fired by his older brother Larry, who also worked there. He worked as a contingency planner for the New Jersey Department of Human Services, a bartender, a puppeteer (performing shows in elementary schools), and a live mosquito sorter for the New Jersey Department of Health.

- Stewart took over as host of *The Daily Show* in 1999. With Stewart at the helm, *The Daily Show* won numerous prestigious awards—including five Emmys and a Peabody—and gained national recognition. In June 2004 a survey found that more than 20 percent of young voters got their news from *The Daily Show*, and a Brookings Institute poll conducted 10 years later found that Stewart was considered more trustworthy than MSNBC to provide accurate news.

*Stewart interviews President Barack Obama in 2010.*

# Grover's Mill's Martians

*Have you heard? Aliens once invaded a small town in New Jersey!*

*Left: Orson Welles in action during the October 1938 broadcast.*

*Below: A Depression-era family gathers around the radio. Welles's 1938 "emergency" radio broadcast about aliens landing in New Jersey set off a panic.*

had landed in rural Grover's Mill. The meteorite was a metal cylinder from another planet. Quick as you could say "flying saucer," New Jersey was facing death and destruction as the American military fell back helpless before the mighty Martian death rays. Or so the story went...

## The Broadcast

"Ladies and gentlemen, I have a grave announcement to make. Incredible as it may seem, both observations of science and the evidence of our eyes lead to the inescapable assumption that those strange beings that landed in the New Jersey farmlands tonight are the vanguard of an invading army from the planet Mars."

On October 30, 1938, when those stunning words came over the radio, millions of Americans in the audience believed they were hearing an official news broadcast from Intercontinental Radio News. Regular programming had been interrupted with a live report from New Jersey, where a strange meteorite

Left: For a few harrowing hours in 1938, many New Jerseyans wondered if flying saucers had invaded their state.

## Martians in New Jersey?!

Not exactly. It was all actually part of Orson Welles's famous *War of the Worlds* radio broadcast, one of the greatest practical jokes ever played on an audience. Since it was the night before Halloween, Welles and his radio theater company adapted H. G. Wells's *War of the Worlds* (a story about an invasion of hostile aliens from Mars) into a scary—and very realistic—radio play. Although it seems silly today, at the time, the program sounded completely authentic, and Americans were in a panic over it.

The show began as a music program—peppered with "flash bulletins" that told the story of a Martian takeover. The use of real locations in the bulletins

Above: British sculptor Michael Condron built this alien in 1998 to celebrate the 100-year anniversary of H. G. Wells's novel War of the Worlds.

*Left: H. G. Wells's* War of the Worlds *was a popular science-fiction story.*

*Right: The* New York Times *reports on the* War of the Worlds *panic.*

**The New York Times**

Copyright, 1938, by The New York Times Company.

Entered as Second-Class Matter, Postoffice, New York, N. Y.

NEW YORK, MONDAY, OCTOBER 31, 1938.

P P

## Radio Listeners in Panic, Taking War Drama as Fact

### Many Flee Homes to Escape 'Gas Raid From Mars'—Phone Calls Swamp Police at Broadcast of Wells Fantasy

A wave of mass hysteria seized thousands of radio listeners throughout the nation between 8:15 and 9:30 o'clock last night when a broadcast of a dramatization of H. G. Wells's fantasy, "The War" and radio stations here and in other cities of the United States and Canada seeking advice on protective measures against the raids.

The program was produced by Mr. Welles and the Mercury Theatre on

convinced unsuspecting listeners that what they were hearing was actually happening. In fact, estimates say that more than a million people thought they were listening to an actual invasion. Concern and panic spread as far west as San Francisco and north into Canada. People went to the hospital convinced that their dizziness and nausea were caused by Martian gas. Others were treated for rashes, rapid heartbeats, hysteria, and shock. Thousands of frightened citizens fled their homes or hid in their cellars. Some even loaded their guns and went hunting for Martians.

## They're Bombing New Jersey!

Even New Jerseyans believed their home state had been attacked. On a single block in Newark, more than 20 families fled their homes with wet handkerchiefs or towels over their faces to protect themselves from poisonous Martian gas. As folks packed up and fled the invasion, churches opened their doors to the newly devout who had come to pray for deliverance from the calamity. And the people in West Orange who chose a more inebriated approach to dealing with the Martian invasion were out of luck when the bartender closed his tavern on Valley Road, believing that everyone had been ordered to evacuate the metropolitan area.

In Maplewood and Orange, newspapers and police were inundated with frantic phone calls. New York and New Jersey State Police had to send out messages via their Teletypes and shortwave radios that

the invasion was fictional. But when Welles broadcast a "bulletin" about the mobilization of 7,000 National Guardsmen in New Jersey, the state armories were overwhelmed by calls from reporting officers and guardsmen.

With today's 24-hour news and access to the Internet, it's easy to think that only the gullible would be fooled by the broadcast, but regular citizens weren't the only ones taken in. In fact, the head of the Department of Geology at Princeton University and another distinguished professor bought it too. Early in the program, when another "bulletin" described a meteorite landing near Princeton, the pair gathered up their equipment. They rushed toward Grover's Mill to search for the alien craft that had been described as "a huge flying object" flaming down to earth.

## Meanwhile, at Grover's Mill…

And then there was the tiny community of Grover's Mill. Surely, because its inhabitants could see for themselves that the Martians and the U.S. Army were nowhere in sight, they weren't fooled by the broadcast.

Not so fast. At the beginning of the broadcast that night, the town was nearly deserted. But by 8:30 p.m. crowds were everywhere, and it was difficult to tell what was going on. Local switchboards were jammed with worried callers. Some citizens pulled out guns, ready for a standoff with the aliens. Fortunately, the only casualty was a farmer's water tower that was mistaken for a Martian spaceship.

Many wondered why a sleepy rural town was chosen as the site for the interplanetary war. The answer was simple. Playwright Howard Koch, who wrote the script, closed his eyes and aimed his pencil point at a map of New Jersey. When the pencil point landed at Grover's Mill, so did the Martians.

## Post-Invasion

Fifty years after the supposed invasion, the story still hadn't been forgotten in New Jersey. In 1988 a six-foot-tall bronze monument was erected in Van Nest Park, near Grover's Mill Pond in West Windsor Township, to mark the place where the aliens first "landed." The face of the monument includes depictions of a Martian craft, Orson Welles performing from his script, and a family listening to the radio. At the dedication Douglas R. Forrester, head of the War of the Worlds Commemorative Committee, gave a speech that touched on the reactions of the residents in Grover's Mill and West

Windsor Township on the night that the Martians "invaded." They were, he explained, just like everyone else at the time: "Some were perplexed, some were amused, and some were alarmed." Ten years later in 1998, a "Martian Ball" was held to celebrate the sixtieth anniversary of the event. And even in the 21st century, fans still flock to visit the monument that celebrates one of the scariest Halloween stories ever told.

*Above: Grover's Mill continues to capitalize on its alien heritage with souvenirs like Martian Eggs.*

*Right: A monument in Grover's Mill, New Jersey, memorializes the fictional Martian landing site.*

# Dino-mite!

*You could say that New Jersey is the birthplace of dinomania (or "vertebrate paleontology," if you're feeling bookish). Why? It's a little-known fact that the first nearly complete dinosaur skeleton was found here in 1858.*

## Hadrosaurus Hunting

Eighty million years ago, New Jersey and eastern Pennsylvania were home to the mighty Hadrosaurus. These duck-billed dinosaurs grew to be approximately 10 feet tall, measured about 25 feet long, weighed from 6 to 8 tons, and dined on plants. One particular Hadrosaurus found its way to what is now Haddonfield, New Jersey, where its body came to be buried under lots and lots of marl, a type of mud that's perfect for preserving dinosaurs.

In the 1830s, local farmer John Hopkins uncovered some unusually large bones in a marl pit. Hopkins and his workers had no idea what they had stumbled on. They treated the bones like, well, bones, and gave them away to be used as doorstops and window jams. Twenty years later in 1858, William Parker Foulke, a member of the Academy of Natural Sciences, spent a summer in Haddonfield. When he heard about the old discovery of the giant bones, he put together his own team to do some digging.

*Joseph Leidy*

## Pay Dirt

Foulke's team soon hit a big bone bonanza. They unearthed 49 bones and teeth that turned out to be the first nearly complete dinosaur skeleton. For the first time, scientists could get a good look at what a whole dinosaur had looked like (minus the skin and muscles, of course). Foulke contacted Dr. Joseph Leidy, a renowned vertebrate paleontologist and professor at the University of Pennsylvania, as well as a fellow member of the Academy of Natural Sciences. Astounded by the creature's structural similarity to both lizards and birds, Leidy immediately recognized it as a dinosaur and christened it *Hadrosaurus foulki*, or "Foulke's bulky lizard." Thanks to Foulke and Leidy, scientists now had the hard evidence they needed to prove the existence of dinosaurs.

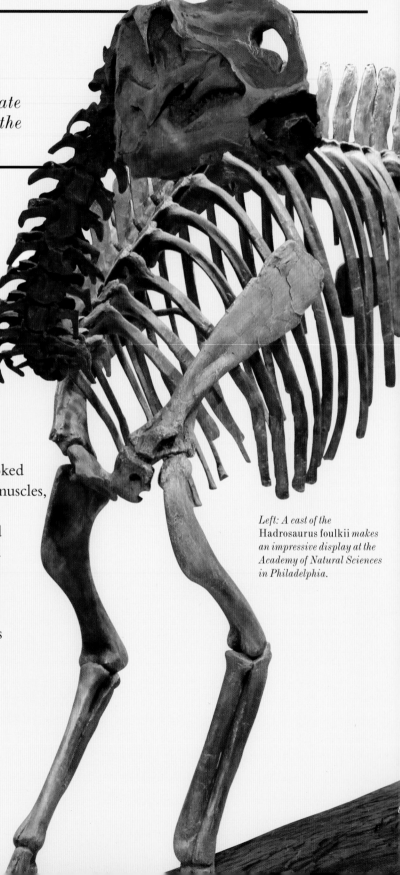

*Left: A cast of the Hadrosaurus foulkii makes an impressive display at the Academy of Natural Sciences in Philadelphia.*

It was the breakthrough they had been looking for.

In 1868 the bones were mounted and sent to the Academy of Natural Sciences at Drexel University in Philadelphia, where they've been ever since. A mounted version made from plaster casts of the original bones is still on display there today.

## Making It Official

In 1988 students at Strawbridge Elementary School in Westmont (near Haddonfield) led the charge to make the Hadrosaurus the official dinosaur of New Jersey. It took three years of wrangling, but the students' efforts paid off in 1991, when the dinosaur was officially adopted by the state. Three years later, the National Park Service designated the discovery site as a National Historic Landmark.

*Left: A statue in Haddonfield commemorates Foulke's historic find.*

*Right: A plaque marks the spot of the dinosaur bone discovery in Haddonfield.*

### HADROSAURUS FOULKII

IN A MARL PIT ON THE JOHN E. HOPKINS FARM IN OCTOBER 1858, THE WORLD'S FIRST NEARLY COMPLETE DINOSAUR SKELETON WAS UNEARTHED BY WILLIAM PARKER FOULKE. THE FIND WAS ADJACENT TO THIS POINT. THIS WAS ALSO THE FIRST DINOSAUR SKELETON TO EVER BE MOUNTED. THE BONES REPRESENTED A 25 FOOT, 7-8 TON HERBIVOROUS HADROSAURUS (REPTILE). ITS HEIGHT PROBABLY RANGED FROM 6-10 FEET AT THE HIPS. SOME 55 OF AN ESTIMATED 80 BONES WERE DISCOVERED. THIS CREATURE LIVED 70-80 MILLION YEARS AGO DURING THE CRETACEOUS PERIOD AT THE END OF THE DINOSAUR AGE.

THIS SITE WAS DEVELOPED IN 1984 AS AN EAGLE SCOUT PROJECT BY CHRISTOPHER BREES, TROOP 65.
MAJOR PROJECT FUNDING BY THE
ACADEMY OF NATURAL SCIENCES, PHILADELPHIA, PA.

# Picture Credits

# The Last Page

**FELLOW BATHROOM READERS:**

The fight for good bathroom reading should never be taken loosely—
we must do our duty and sit firmly for what we believe in, even while
the rest of the world is taking potshots at us. We'll be brief. Now that we've proven we're
not simply a flush-in-the-pan, we invite you to take the plunge: Sit Down and Be Counted!
Log on to www.bathroomreader.com and earn a permanent spot on the BRI honor roll!

If you like reading our books...
VISIT THE BRI'S WEB SITE!
*www.bathroomreader.com*

• Visit "The Throne Room"—a great place to read!
• Receive our irregular newsletters via email.
• Order additional *Bathroom Readers*.
• Read our blog.

*Go with the Flow...*

Well, we're out of space, and when you've gotta go,
you've gotta go. Tanks for all your support. Hope to
hear from you soon. Meanwhile, remember...

*Keep on flushin'!*